Censorship

Look for these and other books in the Lucent
Overview series:

Censorship

by Bradley Steffens

LUCENT
BOOKS

UCENT Overview Series

Library of Congress Cataloging-in-Publication Data

Steffens, Bradley, 1956–
    Censorship / by Bradley Steffens.
        p.   cm. — (Overview series)
    Includes bibliographical references and index.
    Summary: Explores various issues involving censorship,
including civil liberties, obscenity, and the role of government.
    ISBN 1-56006-166-9 (lib. ed. : alk. paper)
    1. Censorship—Juvenile literature.   2. Censorship—United
States—Juvenile literature.   [1. Censorship.]   I. Title.
II. Series: Lucent overview series.
Z657.S825   1996
363.3'1—dc20   95–13424
                                                        CIP
                                                         AC

Copyright © 1996 by Lucent Books, Inc.
P.O. Box 289011, San Diego, CA 92198-9011
Printed in the U.S.A.

For Millie,
whose words of support
encouraged me as I wrote this book

Contents

Introduction

FROM THE BEGINNING of history, people have recognized the power of words to influence lives and shape events. Usually this power is a good thing. A free exchange of ideas has led to progress in religion, the arts, science, and politics. Many of history's most important figures are remembered not only for what they did, but also for what they said. Moses, Shakespeare, Galileo, Jefferson—these are just a few of the people whose words have enlightened and inspired countless people, enriching civilization as a whole.

Unfortunately history has shown that words can be used for ill as well as for good, to destroy lives as well as to enhance them. It all depends on the user. For example, Adolf Hitler used a gift for public speaking and a well-organized propaganda campaign to discredit his critics and rally support for his plan to rid Europe of Jews, Gypsies, and members of other minority groups. Hitler's politics of hatred cost more than six million innocent people their lives. Mindful of the important role propaganda played in Hitler's murderous regime, the postwar government of Germany banned all expression that promoted the Nazi Party or its philosophy of racism and hatred. This ban remains in effect today.

(Opposite page) The authors of the Declaration of Independence aspired to create a document that would protect the freedoms of all Americans. Their creation stands as a testimony to the power of words to shape history.

The German government's ban on Nazi propaganda is an act of censorship—the suppression of words, pictures, or other forms of expression because their content is deemed harmful. Many people believe it makes sense to censor some expression. Since expressive activity occurs in public, these people reason, it is subject to the same rules and laws that govern other types of public conduct. If expression puts people in danger or threatens society as a whole, it should be censored.

Gifted public speakers throughout history have used words to shape national philosophies. Adolf Hitler (center) is among those who have used their talents to encourage Nazi racism and hatred.

Other people disagree. They believe that censorship presents a danger that is worse than any problem that expression itself can cause. Censorship restricts the flow of ideas, depriving people of the information they need to maintain an open society. Benjamin Franklin, who was an author and a publisher in addition to being an American patriot, summed up this belief when he wrote, "They that can give up essential liberty to obtain a little temporary safety deserve neither liberty nor safety."

A poll conducted by NBC News on August 10, 1994, found that 77 percent of those surveyed believed that the government should be allowed to restrict some expression. Although most Americans support some types of censorship, debate continues over how great a danger speech must pose before it should be censored. Clearly, urging a crowd to lynch a person should be forbidden, but what about calling for the overthrow of the government? Should such words be banned as well?

These are questions over which reasonable people—even Supreme Court justices—disagree. They are the issues this book is designed to explore.

A strong opponent of censorship, Benjamin Franklin opposed the sacrifice of liberty for temporary safety.

1

A Legacy of Restraint

CENSORSHIP IS AS old as language itself. Many ancient people believed that words held special powers. They reasoned that such powers had to be controlled for the good of the community. For example, many Native Americans believed that names held magic powers. They thought that a person who knew another person's name held power over the person whose name was known. The one who knew the name could use that power to harm the other person or his or her tribe. To avoid this fate, these Native Americans were forbidden from speaking their names in public.

In many cultures speaking the names of gods and spirits was also taboo. For example, the third commandment, one of ten laws that Moses, a leader of the Jews, presented to his people around 1250 B.C., forbade the speaking of the name of God, except in prayer or during a religious ceremony. "Thou shalt not take the name of the Lord thy God in vain," read this commandment. This ancient law is still observed by devout Jews, Christians, and Muslims, all of whom consider it to be part of their scriptures, or sacred writings.

The third commandment is not the only one that limits speech. The ninth commandment

(Opposite page) Moses presents the Ten Commandments to the Jewish people. The laws contained in the commandments forbid certain types of speech and serve as a model for modern laws restricting false statements.

declares, "Thou shalt not bear false witness against thy neighbor." The purpose of this law was to protect members of Moses' tribe from being falsely accused of evil deeds. Adopted by the Christian church and spread throughout the world, the ninth commandment served as the basis of modern laws restricting false statements such as perjury, slander, and libel.

The Jews were not the only ancient people to restrict speech. The Greeks also placed limits on what was said, written, or performed in theaters. In fact, one of the greatest thinkers and teachers of ancient Greece, Socrates, was censored by the government in 399 B.C. Socrates was charged with corrupting the youth of Athens because he taught his students to challenge conventional thinking. Socrates did not believe his words were false or harmful. He refused to renounce his teachings or even to accept the punishment of exile from the

As a philosopher and teacher, Socrates (center) often discussed his beliefs before an audience. When the government censored his speech in 399 B.C., Socrates refused to renounce his teachings and was sentenced to death.

city. The great philosopher was sentenced to death. He was given a cup containing the deadly juice of the hemlock plant, which he drank without fear. His death remains one of the most stirring protests against censorship in the history of the world.

The coming of the censor

The Romans, who conquered Greece in the first century B.C. and ruled an empire that contained more than 100 million people, also censored speech. Indeed, the word *censorship* is derived from the title of the Roman official responsible for enforcing speech codes: the censor.

The office of the censor was created in 443 B.C. by the *comitia centuriata*, an assembly of Roman leaders. At first the duty of the censor was to count the number of Roman citizens. This count, known as a census, was used by the Roman government to collect taxes, regulate voting, and raise armies. Slowly the powers of the censor grew. He became responsible for setting standards of behavior and manners within the empire.

The domain of the censor encompassed not only what Roman citizens did, but also what they said and wrote. Even speeches by members of the Roman Senate were subject to review by the censor. A senator who breached the censor's standards could be removed from office or even banished from the city.

In the fourth century A.D. the Roman Empire adopted Christianity as the official state religion. Christian laws became the laws of Rome. The censor enforced not only Roman speech codes, but also those of the Ten Commandments.

A righteous censor

About one hundred years later Germanic tribes living in the western half of the empire seized control of the lands on which they lived. The

Members of the Roman Senate were required to obey the censor's standards. Failure to do so resulted in expulsion from office or exile from the city.

leaders of these tribes established their own governments, naming themselves as kings. Most of these kings were Christians, so they adopted Christian law as their own. As Christians, the European monarchs revered the pope, the head of the Roman Catholic Church. Medieval Christians believed the pope to be God's representative on earth. Because the pope was inspired by God, Christians believed, he was infallible, or perfect, in his judgment, actions, and decrees. His word was law for kings and commoners alike.

The pope replaced the Roman censor as the arbiter of speech in Europe. He had the power to suppress any words he believed were immoral or untrue. For example, a sermon or book that referred to God but conflicted with the pope's beliefs could be found to have taken "the name of the Lord . . . in vain." Indeed, any writing or speech that challenged church doctrine could be ruled a heresy, or false teaching.

The pope set the standards for speech in the Middle Ages, but he did not have to enforce these codes himself. He had the support of bishops, cardinals, priests, and nuns in Europe. He also could count on the support of loyal kings and queens, officials within their governments, and church elders. The members of Christendom made up an army of censors.

The Inquisition

Late in the Middle Ages medieval scholars rediscovered the cultures of the ancient Greeks and

During the Middle Ages the pope established the standards for speech in Europe. As head of the Roman Catholic Church, his word was obeyed by both nobles and peasants.

Romans. Interest in secular, or nonreligious, learning grew. This movement, later known as the Renaissance, concerned members of the Catholic Church. They feared that such learning would lead people away from the life of faith. Some zealous, or passionate, Christians believed an evil spirit named Satan was behind the surge in secular study. It was all part of the evil one's plan to destroy Christianity, they reasoned. They saw a battle taking shape between good and evil, truth and falsehood. This conflict would be fought in the schools, churches, and universities of Europe. It was to be largely a war of words.

The army of Christian censors charged into action. They scoured books and papers, searching for evidence of heresy, insults against God, and other crimes against the church. They took notes at speeches, wrote down rumors, and asked scholars about their colleagues. Thousands of authors, speakers, scholars, and artists were arrested and questioned about their work. If they denied wrongdoing, they often were tortured until they confessed. Many of those found guilty were killed. This period of persecution and censorship is known today as the Inquisition.

Zealous Christian censors sent thousands of authors, scholars, and artists to their deaths during the Inquisition.

The printing press invented by Johannes Gutenberg (left) allowed Johann Fust (right) and his partner, Peter Schöffer, to produce more copies of the Bible than could ever have been copied by hand.

As the war between scholars and censors raged across Europe, two businessmen in Mainz, Germany—Johann Fust and Peter Schöffer—began to offer copies of the Bible for sale in 1455. At the time Fust and Schöffer's efforts did not seem especially important. After all the Bible was the most widely sold book in Europe. Nor were Fust and Schöffer's actions controversial. Every Christian, from the pope to the humblest parishioner, believed the Bible to be the Word of God. Selling it only brought greater glory to the Lord.

Fust and Schöffer's venture was significant, however. What was important was how their Bible had been made. Unlike every other book manufactured in Europe up to that time, Fust and Schöffer's Bible had not been copied by hand. It had been produced on a machine devised by an ingenious German artisan named Johannes Gutenberg. That machine was the printing press, and it was destined to change the course of censorship forever.

Before the invention of the printing press, censorship was simple. Most communication—public as well as private—was oral. To silence an idea, all a censor had to do was silence the speaker. The simplest way of doing this was by sentencing the speaker to death. Unless someone transcribes the speaker's words, his or her ideas would be buried along with his or her physical remains.

Even if a person's words were written down, however, a censor still could suppress them easily. This is because the only way to reproduce a person's sayings or writings was to copy them by hand, which took a great deal of time. Using a quill pen, a highly skilled copyist needed five months to copy a single book.

The revolution of the press

The printing press changed all that. With a press a person could produce more pages in an hour than a scribe could copy in a month. "There has been discovered in Germany a wonderful new method for the production of books," wrote a French scholar named Guillaume Fichet in 1470, "and those who have mastered the art are taking it from Mainz out into the world. . . . The light of this discovery will spread from Germany to all parts of the world."

Fichet was right. All across Europe artisans began to copy Gutenberg's methods and machinery. By 1500 more than one thousand printers had set up shop. Book production soared. Historians estimate that when Fust and Schöffer first offered the Gutenberg Bible for sale in 1455, the libraries of Europe contained fewer than one million books. By 1500 that number had soared to ten million. Less than fifty years after Gutenberg's breakthrough, a scribe in Venice reported that his city was "stuffed with books."

The invention of the printing press made it extremely difficult for governments to censor written materials. Because a printer could produce and distribute numerous copies of a book, the work could be seen by thousands of readers before it reached a censor.

Because of the printing press, a written account of a person's thoughts could be in the hands of hundreds, even thousands, of readers before a censor ever found out about it. This fact upset the monarchs of Europe. They worried that criticism of them and their governments could spread through their kingdoms like wildfire, turning the people against them and making the task of governing more difficult. For example, criticism about the conduct of a war could make it harder for a king to raise an army. Statements that a queen was not the rightful heir to the throne could make it easier for a rival to lead a rebellion against her. The solution, the monarchs thought, was simple: control the presses, and a leader could control public opinion.

European monarchs sought to control printing presses by requiring printers to obtain permission before publishing any work. This measure reinforced a government's ability to censor materials that criticized the monarchy.

In 1521 the king of Germany declared that all printers had to obtain a license before they could go into business. Printers also had to show anything they planned to publish to the government before publication. If a government censor believed the work would hurt the monarchy, the printer would not be allowed to publish it. This kind of censorship is known today as prior restraint.

Other European monarchs followed the example of the German king. In 1538 King Henry VIII of England declared that printers in his country had to obtain permission before publishing any work. In 1561 the French monarchy outlawed the publication of material that criticized the government. Printers who violated this decree once were whipped. Those found guilty a second time were hanged. Between 1600 and 1756 more than eight hundred French writers, publishers, and booksellers were imprisoned or executed for criticizing the government.

In England prior restraint was enforced by the printers themselves. They formed an organization called Stationers Company to register all printed works. Members of the Stationers Company routinely searched print shops and warehouses for books or pamphlets that criticized the monarchy. For example, the Stationers Company discovered a play by William Prynne that made fun of King Charles I and Queen Henrietta Maria. The royal soldiers arrested Prynne and burned copies of the offending work.

A period of freedom

Many English writers and publishers opposed the policy of prior restraint. In 1641 one man, Samuel Pecke, openly defied the royal edict. Even though the British king, Charles I, had forbidden newspapers to print stories about his government, Pecke began to publish a weekly newspaper entitled *The Heads of Several Proceedings in This Present Parliament*. He described how members of the British Parliament, led by Oliver Cromwell, were demanding a greater voice in the affairs of the state. Support for Cromwell's movement was so great that King Charles was unable to stop the publication of Pecke's newspaper. Seeing Pecke go unpunished, other publishers began to print newspapers that described relations between Parliament and the king.

In 1642 the dispute between Cromwell and the king reached the breaking point. Civil war broke out. With their resources committed to the war, neither King Charles nor Oliver Cromwell had

King Charles I of England issued a royal edict forbidding newspapers from printing information about his government.

the power to control the press, and English printers were free to publish whatever they wished.

Many people welcomed this newfound freedom of the press. One of its most eloquent supporters was the great English poet John Milton. In a 1644 book entitled *Areopagitica*, Milton maintained that society had nothing to fear from a free press, because good ideas will always triumph over bad ones:

> And though all the winds of doctrine were let loose to play upon the earth, so Truth be in the field, we do . . . by licensing and prohibiting . . . misdoubt [Truth's] strength. Let [Truth] and Falsehood grapple; who ever knew Truth put to the worst in a free and open encounter.

After seven years of war Cromwell's forces finally defeated the king's army. On January 30, 1649, King Charles was beheaded. Many people assumed that English censorship would die with the monarchy. They were wrong. Soon after forming a new government, Cromwell took steps to censor the press. Like the monarchs he succeeded, Cromwell required printers to obtain licenses from the government and to submit their works before publication.

Printers revolt against censorship

Having briefly enjoyed freedom of the press, many British printers resented Cromwell's actions. Some defied the Lord Protector of England, as Cromwell called himself. These bold publishers were promptly jailed. Others lobbied, or attempted to influence, members of Parliament for greater freedom. Still others packed up their presses and moved to the British colonies on a faraway continent known as North America.

One such publisher was Benjamin Harris. Once jailed for violating English sedition laws, Harris fled to Massachusetts in 1686. Four years later he

English newspapers kept the public well informed during the struggle between Oliver Cromwell (pictured) and King Charles I.

King Charles I is readied for execution. Many printers believed Cromwell's victory would mark the end of English censorship. However, Cromwell continued censorship of the press as head of the new government.

founded North America's first newspaper, *Publick Occurrences Both Forreign and Domestick.* Starved for news, the colonists snapped up copies of Harris's paper. The governor of the colony, however, was not pleased with the new publication. After reading a copy, he issued an edict calling for the "Disallowance of said Pamphlet." The first issue of *Publick Occurrences* was also the last.

The next American colonist to publish a newspaper was John Campbell of Boston. Encouraged by the fact that the Licensing Act, a British law that restricted the press, had expired, Campbell founded the *Boston News-Letter* in 1704. Campbell took care to avoid offending the colonial governor. He reprinted stories that appeared in

The Stamp Act of 1765 placed a new tax on publications and legal documents. Newspapers such as the Pennsylvania Journal and Weekly Advertiser *could not afford the new fees and temporarily went out of business.*

Samuel Adams, one of the leaders of the American Revolution, praised newspapers for their protests against British taxation.

newspapers that arrived by ship from England then added local news from the Boston area. The governor did not object to the contents of Campbell's paper. The *Boston News-Letter* was a huge success.

Encouraged by Campbell's efforts, printers in major colonial cities began publishing newspapers. Unlike Campbell, some of the publishers criticized the government. For example, when Parliament passed the Stamp Act in 1765, placing a new tax on publications and legal documents, several colonial newspapers attacked the action. Because of these protests Parliament repealed the tax in March 1766. A similar event occurred one year later. Parliament passed the Townshend Acts, taxing tea, glass, lead, paint, and paper imports, as well as suspending the Massachusetts Assembly. Again, American newspapers reproached the British government for its actions. As a result, Parliament repealed the tax on all items except for tea and restored the assembly.

Looking back at this period of protest, Samuel Adams, one of the leaders of the American Revolution, wrote, "The Revolution was effected [accomplished] before the war commenced . . . in the hearts and minds of the people. . . . This radical change in the principles, opinions, sentiments, and affections of the people, was the real American Revolution."

"Informations from the Press"

A key figure in the "real American Revolution" was a pamphleteer named Thomas Paine. In his most famous pamphlet, *Common Sense*, Paine called for an end to the so-called fraud of the British monarchy. Published in January 1776, *Common Sense* sold 120,000 copies in just three months. One out of every twenty-five people living in the American colonies at the time owned a copy of Paine's essay. His words reached "the

Thomas Paine, author of Common Sense, *was an instrumental figure in the American Revolution. His famous pamphlet sold 120,000 copies in only three months.*

hearts and minds" of thousands more who borrowed the pamphlet or heard it discussed. Less than six months after *Common Sense* appeared, the American colonists declared their independence from Britain.

The war for American independence, the Revolutionary War, dragged on for eight years. During this time Paine and others published tracts, or political writings, designed to lift the spirits of the rebels. "These are the times that try men's souls," wrote Paine in the winter of 1780, while with Washington's army in New Jersey. Such inspirational words had a profound effect on the outcome of the war, according to a writer who called himself "a Countryman." In an essay that appeared in the March 12, 1786, edition of the *Providence Gazette*, the anonymous essayist wrote: "Had it not been for the continual informations from the Press, a junction of all the people on this northern continent . . . would have been scarcely conceivable."

A guarantee of freedom

The American colonists won their freedom in 1783. As the leaders of the American Revolution began to form a new government, they looked for ways to ensure that citizens of the new nation would be free to criticize the government both in speech and in the press. The delegates of the First Continental Congress believed that a free press was needed to keep government from becoming corrupt or too powerful. In a resolution, they declared:

> The importance of [a free press] consists, besides the advancement of truth, science, morality and arts in general, in its diffusion of liberal sentiment on the administration of government, its ready communication of thoughts between subjects, and its consequential promotion of union among them, whereby oppressive officials are shamed or intimi-

George Mason, author of the Virginia Declaration of Rights, petitioned for a bill of rights to be added to the Constitution to ensure that the right to free speech and free press was guaranteed by law.

dated into more honorable and just modes of conducting affairs.

Some American patriots, especially George Mason of Virginia, believed that the right to free speech and a free press needed to be guaranteed by law. The author of the Virginia Declaration of Rights, Mason called for a similar bill of rights to be added to the U.S. Constitution. He urged legislators of the various states to refuse to approve the Constitution unless a bill of rights was added to the document.

Other leaders, such as James Madison and Alexander Hamilton, disagreed with Mason. A bill of rights was not necessary, they argued, because the Constitution did not give the government the power to deprive people of their rights. "Why declare that things shall not be done which there is no power to do?" asked Alexander Hamilton in *The Federalist* papers. "Why, for instance, should it be said, that the liberty of the press shall not be restrained, when no power is given by which restrictions may be imposed?"

Not everyone was convinced by the arguments expressed in *The Federalist* papers. Both John Adams and Thomas Jefferson wrote from abroad, urging the supporters of the Constitution to adopt a bill of rights. "A bill of rights is what the people are entitled to against every government on earth, general or particular, and what no just government should refuse or rest on inference," wrote Jefferson.

The First Amendment

Eventually the supporters of what is now called the Bill of Rights prevailed. James Madison even volunteered to write the guarantees he felt were unnecessary. Using the most sweeping language

James Madison (left) and Alexander Hamilton (right) felt that a bill of rights was unnecessary. They argued that the Constitution did not provide government with the power to deprive people of their rights, and therefore additional guarantees were unneeded.

Thomas Jefferson insisted that citizens were entitled to a bill of rights. He further asserted that a fair government would not refuse such a measure.

he could think of, the future president of the United States began to compose what was to become the First Amendment to the Constitution: "Congress shall make no law abridging [diminishing] . . . freedom of speech, or of the press," he wrote. On December 15, 1791, Virginia became the eleventh state to ratify the Bill of Rights, making it part of the Constitution. Freedom of speech and of the press became the law of the land.

———————— **2** ————————

Rights in Conflict

————————

THE BELIEF THAT individual rights and freedoms—such as the rights to free speech and a free press—must be secured by laws did not originate with George Mason and other supporters of the Bill of Rights. These concepts had been described more than one hundred years earlier by an English philosopher named John Locke.

The son of an attorney, John Locke was born on August 29, 1632, in Wrington, England. He attended Westminster, the leading public school in England at the time. At the age of twenty Locke entered Oxford University, where he studied philosophy, science, and medicine. At the age of thirty-four Locke became the private doctor of Anthony Ashley Cooper, first earl of Shaftesbury, an English nobleman who served in Parliament. Shaftesbury befriended his young doctor, drawing Locke into discussions of history, politics, and government. With Shaftesbury's support, Locke pursued his true talent and passion—philosophy.

The paradox of liberty

In his philosophical writings, Locke often defined issues by describing their opposite. For example, in his essay *Two Treatises on Government* Locke explained the purpose of government by first describing what it would be like to live with-

(Opposite page) The rights of society sometimes conflict with the rights of the individual. An example is when someone is forced to fight in a war that he or she opposes despite the government's decision that the war is in the national interest. This young man burns his draft card in defiance of the Vietnam War.

33

out any government. He called such a condition a "state of nature." In a state of nature, Locke wrote, all people are born with basic, God-given rights. Because there are no laws to restrain people, however, these rights are "very uncertain and constantly exposed to the invasion of others." People who are strong enough to impose their will on others enjoy many rights. Those who are too weak to defend their rights enjoy very few.

To ensure the rights of everyone—weak and strong alike—people band together to form a society. They enter into what Locke called a social compact, or contract, with other people. They agree to give up some of their individual freedoms in exchange for greater security for the rights that are most important to them. They replace a society that rules by power with one that rules by law. The purpose of government, Locke concluded, is to secure individual rights.

Locke and the Constitution

Locke's ideas had a profound effect on the generation of Americans that revolted against British rule. As they composed the documents that founded their new nation, American patriots echoed Locke's words. "We hold these truths to be self-evident," wrote Thomas Jefferson in the Declaration of Independence, "that all men are . . . endowed by their Creator with certain unalienable [unchangeable] Rights. . . . That to secure these rights, Governments are instituted among Men." In the preamble to the Constitution of the United States, the members of the Constitutional Convention wrote:

> We the People of the United States, in Order to form a more perfect Union, establish Justice, insure domestic Tranquility . . . and secure the Blessings of Liberty to ourselves and our Posterity, do ordain and establish this Constitution for the United States of America.

The writings of English philosopher John Locke greatly influenced the American Revolution. His philosophies about government are reflected in the Declaration of Independence and the Constitution.

Although faded with age, the preamble to the Constitution continues to uphold John Locke's belief that the purpose of government is to secure individual rights.

Locke's writings on government contain a paradox, a statement that seems to contradict itself, yet is true. According to Locke the only way to secure individual rights is to establish the rule of law, but the only way to establish the rule of law is to give up some individual rights. This is the paradox of liberty.

Because a paradox appears contradictory, people often pay attention to one part of it and ignore the other. For example, people who prize individual rights above all else tend to concentrate on the idea that government exists to protect their rights. They forget that when they enter into the social compact that makes government possible, they automatically forfeit some rights. Likewise, people who value an orderly society tend to focus on the belief that people must forfeit some of their

Delegates of the Constitutional Convention compose the U.S. Constitution. While the document secured individual rights, it also took away some liberties in order to establish the rule of law.

rights to preserve the rule of law. They forget that the goal of government is to secure individual rights, not to take them away. By themselves, neither view is correct; but taken together, both are true. That is the nature of a paradox.

Trading one right for another

Even highly educated people sometimes ignore the paradoxical nature of liberty. One such person was George Hay, an eighteenth-century American lawyer. Focusing on the belief that government exists to protect individual rights, Hay maintained that the First Amendment means exactly what it says. "The word 'freedom' has meaning," he wrote. "It is either absolute, that is, exempt from all law, or it is qualified, that is, regulated by law." The freedom to speak could not be regulated by law under the Constitution, Hay reasoned, otherwise the "Amendment which declared that Congress shall make no law to abridge the freedom of the press . . . is the grossest absurdity that ever was conceived by the human mind."

Hugo Black, a twentieth-century associate justice of the Supreme Court, agreed with Hay:

> Madison and the other Framers of the First Amendment, able men that they were, wrote in language they earnestly believed could never be misunderstood: "Congress shall make *no law* . . . abridging freedom . . . of the press."

Another twentieth-century Supreme Court associate justice, Felix Frankfurter, disagreed with Hay and Black. "There are those who find in the Constitution a wholly unfettered [unrestrained] right of expression," he wrote in the 1951 case of *Dennis et al. v. United States*. "Such literalness treats the words of the Constitution as though they were found on a piece of out-worn parchment instead of being words that have called into being a nation with a past to be preserved for the future," he observed. The purpose of the Bill of Rights, in Frankfurter's opinion, was to preserve legal guarantees "inherited from our English ancestors." These guarantees, he pointed out, had never been absolute. Instead, he wrote, they "had from time immemorial been subject to certain well-recognized exceptions." For this reason, Frankfurter concluded, "Free speech is subject to prohibition of those abuses of expression which a civilized society may forbid."

Personal liberty and the social compact

Associate justice Robert H. Jackson, who served on the Supreme Court at the same time as Frankfurter, agreed with his colleague. In his dissent in an important censorship case, *Terminiello v. Chicago*, 1949, Jackson noted that too much personal liberty erodes the social compact that makes government possible. He warned that an extreme emphasis on individual rights would cause a breakdown of the social order:

> The choice is not between order and liberty. It is between liberty with order, and anarchy without either. There is a danger that, if the Court does not temper its . . . logic with a little practical wisdom, it will convert the constitutional Bill of Rights into a suicide pact.

Usually the rights that people are willing to give up to create the rule of law matter less to them than the rights they gain through orderly government. For example, anyone who owns a car might be said to have the right to drive it whenever, wherever, and at whatever speed he or she wishes. If everyone drove as they wished, however, the roadways would be extremely dangerous. Most people gladly forfeit the freedom to drive in a state of nature in exchange for the safety they gain by having traffic laws.

Forfeiting individual rights

Sometimes, however, people are required to forfeit rights that are important to them. For example, a person may be compelled to give up his freedom—and even his life—to fight in a war. Someone who refuses to serve in the army when drafted can be jailed. Society is willing to deprive a person of the most basic individual rights because the safety and the rights of the entire group may depend on the outcome of the war. In such cases the rights of the group prevail over the rights of the individual.

Not all conflicts over rights pit the rights of the individual against the rights of the group, however. Sometimes they pit the rights of one person against the rights of another. Occasionally both of the individual rights in conflict are guaranteed by the Bill of Rights. For example, a publisher might decide

to print details about an upcoming trial. Such pre-trial publicity could make it hard for the court to find jurors who have not formed an opinion about the case. This would infringe on the defendant's Sixth Amendment right to a "public trial, by an impartial jury." However, limiting what the publisher can print about the case would infringe on the publisher's First Amendment right to a free press.

Although demonstrators are free to protest wars they feel are unjust, they can be jailed if they are called to serve in the military and refuse.

The Supreme Court

The framers of the Constitution foresaw that conflicts would arise involving the various rights guaranteed by the Constitution. Such disputes, they reasoned, should be decided by a panel of judges. In Article III of the Constitution, they wrote:

> The judicial Power of the United States, shall be vested in one supreme Court, and in such inferior Courts as the Congress may from time to time ordain and establish. . . . The judicial Power shall extend to all Cases, in Law and Equity, arising under this Constitution.

As the nation's highest court, the Supreme Court has final say in disputes over conflicting rights guaranteed by the Constitution.

According to this article, the Supreme Court is the final arbiter of disputes that arise over conflicting rights guaranteed by the Constitution. It is the duty of the Supreme Court, wrote Alexander Hamilton in the *Federalist,* paper number 78, to void laws that conflict with the Constitution. John Marshall, the fourth chief justice of the Supreme Court, agreed with Hamilton. In *Marbury v. Madison*, 1803, Marshall wrote, "It is . . . the province and duty of the judicial department to say what the law is."

A person who believes that he or she has been restrained or punished under a law that conflicts with the Constitution has the right to appeal the verdict to a higher court. Sometimes such cases must go all the way to the Supreme Court for a ruling. If the majority of the Court agrees that the law conflicts with the Constitution, it is held to be unconstitutional. With such a ruling, the law is struck down; it can no longer be enforced. If the

Supreme Court sees no conflict with the Constitution, the law is upheld and remains in force.

The justices of the Supreme Court often explain their rulings in written opinions. These opinions serve as guidelines for judges serving in lower courts who might have to rule on similar cases. Written opinions also help legislators draft laws that will survive challenges to their constitutionality. In addition, written opinions help lawyers decide if their clients have grounds for appealing verdicts that go against them.

Limits

In the more than two hundred years since the Constitution was adopted, dozens of laws have been challenged before the Supreme Court on

Chief Justice John Marshall once wrote that "the duty of the judicial department is to say what the law is," thus paving the way for the Supreme Court to act as arbiter in constitutional disputes.

First Amendment grounds. Many of these laws have been struck down as unconstitutional. However, the Court has never accepted the view that the freedoms guaranteed by the First Amendment are "exempt from all law," as George Hay put it. When a speaker infringes on the rights of others, the Court has found, he or she can be censored. "The most stringent [rigid] protection of free speech would not protect a man in falsely shouting fire in a crowded theatre and causing a panic," wrote Justice Oliver Wendell Holmes Jr. in *Schenck v. United States*, 1919, giving just one example of speech that falls outside First Amendment protection.

Justice Holmes's opinion affirms the ancient belief in the power of words. Speech can do much more than sway people's opinions. It can affect their judgment, arouse their emotions, move them to action. Unfortunately, not all speech is harmless. Human beings do not become more humane simply because they decide to express themselves. Evil people can use words to

In the case of Schenck v. United States, *Justice Oliver Wendell Holmes Jr. helped establish that certain types of speech are not protected by the First Amendment.*

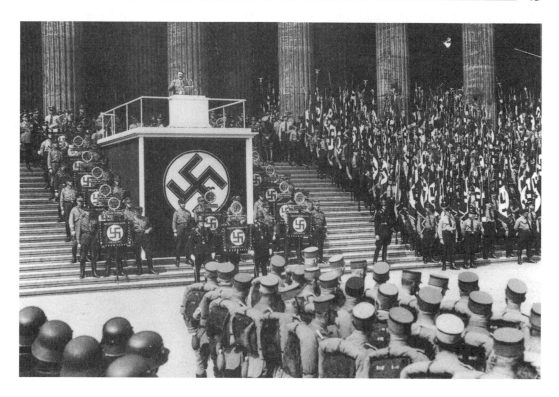

promote evil ends, and they often do. When such expression deprives other people of their rights, Justice Holmes reasoned, the state has the right to restrain, burden, or punish it. Holmes's thinking was shaped by centuries of American and British legal tradition. More than 150 years earlier, Sir William Blackstone, a famous British legal scholar, wrote:

> Every free man has a right to lay what sentiments he pleases before the public . . . but if he publishes what is improper, mischievous, or illegal, he must take the consequences.

The unanimous decision in *Schenck v. United States* made it clear that the First Amendment freedoms of speech and of the press were not absolute. Expression could be punished and even stopped if it conflicted with the public's safety or the nation's right to remain secure. Prior restraint was still forbidden, but censorship was alive and well.

Nearly twenty years after Justice Holmes ruled on the harms that certain types of speech can cause, Germany fell prey to the rhetoric of Adolf Hitler.

KEEP ABORTION LEGAL
MADISON SQUARE
D92
NOT CROSS
BUSH PRO-LIFE
PRO DEATH
GUESS

3

Time, Place, and Manner

WEEK AFTER WEEK in 1991 a group of protesters gathered outside the Aware Woman Center for Choice in Melbourne, Florida. The protesters were part of Rescue America, a national organization opposed to abortion. Some of the protesters held printed leaflets in their hands. Others bore hand-drawn placards. Some brought along bullhorns to amplify their voices. Their goal, they said, was to stop women from going into the clinic to obtain abortions.

As patients walked toward the clinic, the protesters pleaded with them to change their minds about having abortions. If the patients continued toward the door, the protesters' pleas often turned to cries of anguish and finally to shouts of anger. As the doctors inside the clinic performed abortions, the protesters outside sang hymns, chanted slogans, honked car horns, whistled, and shouted through the bullhorns to disrupt the procedures. "Mommy! Don't kill me! They're ripping my arm off!" the protesters sometimes yelled. Some protesters wrote the names of the patients—often along with the word *murderer*—on signs and held them in full view of the patients in the clinic's recovery room.

(Opposite page) The issue of abortion arouses emotional debate among demonstrators. Although the Supreme Court cannot censor demonstrators' speech, it can rule on the constitutionality of the time, place, and manner of the speech.

45

The owner of the clinic, Patricia Windle, believed the protesters were violating the rights of the people who wanted to use the clinic, many of whom were poor. "They are trying to shut off any right to choose for poor women in the area who need medical treatment," said Windle's attorney, Talbot D'Alemberte. In addition, Windle found, the ruckus outside the clinic upset the patients inside. Doctors and nurses reported that the blood pressure of the patients rose during the protests, putting the patients at greater risk.

Windle took the matter to court. She and her lawyers asked circuit court judge Robert B. McGregor to curb the protests. The government, the clinic's lawyers argued, had a duty to protect the rights of the patients. "This is purely an issue of health and public safety," said D'Alemberte.

Attorneys for Judy Madsen and other members of Rescue America disagreed. They believed their clients' rights to free speech were being infringed. They maintained their clients had the right under

the First Amendment to gather on the sidewalk and to discuss the issue of abortion in any manner they saw fit. The fact that patients found the presence of protesters outside the clinic disturbing was no reason to ban the protest, they argued. They quoted from Justice William J. Brennan's majority opinion in *Texas v. Johnson*, 1989:

> If there is a bedrock principle underlying the First Amendment, it is that the Government may not prohibit the expression of an idea simply because society finds the idea itself offensive or disagreeable.

In September 1992 Judge McGregor ruled that the protesters' actions constituted not protest, but harassment. McGregor issued an injunction, or court order, designed to create a buffer zone around the clinic. The injunction barred the protesters from coming within thirty-six feet of the entrance of the clinic. It also forbade the protesters from approaching patients within three hundred feet of the entrance of the clinic "unless such person [the patient] indicates a desire to communicate." In April 1993 Judge McGregor expanded the injunction to ban singing, chanting, honking car horns, or using bullhorns "during surgical procedures and recovery periods."

Ruling against protected speech

The antiabortion activists appealed the judge's ruling on First Amendment grounds. In 1993 the Florida Supreme Court heard the case. In October of that year the court upheld Judge McGregor's ruling. "The First Amendment must yield when protected speech substantially interferes with the normal functioning of a public or private place," stated the court.

Lawyers for Madsen and Rescue America again appealed. In April 1994 the U.S. Supreme Court heard oral arguments in the case. Talbot D'Alemberte argued that the judge's order was aimed at the disruptive nature of the protest, not at its message. "It's not a matter of what's being said," said D'Alembert. "It's what these defendants have done." Speaking from the bench, Justice Antonin Scalia disputed this assertion. "You know what kind of speech you're stopping," Scalia countered. "Any injunction against this group is defacto [in fact] content-directed."

Constitutional limits

The high court announced its decision in *Madsen v. Women's Health Center, Inc.* on June 30, 1994. By a six to three vote, the high court upheld the injunction. The thirty-six-foot buffer zone curtailed speech, Chief Justice William Rehnquist admitted, but such a limit was constitutional because it affected "no more speech than necessary to accomplish the governmental interest at stake." The high court also found that McGregor's noise limits were constitutional. The Court did object to the three-hundred-foot zone, however. An eight-to-one majority held that the Florida judge had exceeded his authority by preventing protesters from approaching people within the larger zone. Only Justice John Paul Stevens maintained that the larger zone was constitutional as well.

In *Madsen v. Women's Health Center, Inc.*, the high court was following guidelines handed down from previous cases about the "time, place, and manner" of expression. In these rulings the high court drew a distinction between the conduct of a communicator and the content of the message. According to the Court the conduct of a communicator can be regulated by the government, even when the content of the message is constitutionally protected. As Richard Conviser, author of *California II Bar/Bri Bar Review*, a reference book for lawyers, put it:

Although an individual's speech may be protected by the Constitution, some conduct can be regulated by the government even if it limits expression.

All speech is conveyed through physical action—whether that action is talking, writing, distributing pamphlets, wearing an arm band, burning a draft card, or burning a building. The fact that the conduct is intended to communicate, and in fact does communicate, cannot immunize it from reasonable government regulation—even though such regulation may incidentally limit communication.

Time

The time at which a person chooses to communicate is an important aspect of the speech-related conduct, according to the Supreme Court. Speech that might be appropriate at one time of day might not be appropriate at another. For example, a speech delivered with a loudspeaker in a park across the street from an apartment building might be perfectly allowable at two in the afternoon. The same speech delivered at two in the morning, however, would be a nuisance.

Demonstrators bicker over the issue of abortion. The timing of their communication is an important factor in determining whether their speech is constitutionally protected.

The timing of the protesters' speech was an important factor in *Madsen v. Women's Health Center, Inc.* Judge McGregor did not ban all singing, chanting, and using bullhorns outside the clinic. He restricted such expression only "during surgical procedures and recovery periods," because those were the times when the expression posed the greatest danger to the patients.

Place

Just as the timing of speech is a factor in whether or not it can be censored, so too is the place where the speech occurs. A demonstration held in a traditional meeting place—such as a public park, a sidewalk, or the steps of a capitol—will receive greater protection under the First Amendment than will the same activity held in front of a military base or a jail. In *United States v. Grace*, 1983, for example, the Supreme Court held that a federal law banning the display of signs or the distribution of leaflets in the United States Supreme Court Building and on its grounds was invalid when applied to people on the sidewalks next to the building. Sidewalks, the Court said, are a public forum. Communication occurring in a public forum, the Court held, is protected by the First Amendment. In the same decision, however, the Court held that the law was valid when applied to people inside the Court building, because courtrooms, hallways, and offices are not a public forum.

In *Madsen v. Women's Health Center, Inc.*, the Supreme Court held that while the sidewalk outside the health center is a public forum, the thirty-six feet around the entrance of the clinic that Judge McGregor set aside as a buffer zone was not. Therefore, the Court found Judge McGregor's injunction to be constitutional.

Manner

The manner in which expression occurs can also be regulated by the government. For example, in *Kovaks v. Cooper*, 1949, the Supreme Court held that a statute prohibiting excessively loud sound trucks was valid. The law did not ban all sound trucks, only those that caused a distur-

Protesters demonstrate on a sidewalk outside of the Capitol. The Supreme Court has determined that sidewalks, unlike building interiors and offices, are public places where freedom of expression is protected.

bance. It was on this basis that Judge McGregor felt free to limit the horn honking, chanting, singing, and the use of bullhorns outside the Aware Woman Center for Choice.

Considering content

While judges and lawmakers may restrict the conduct of speakers, they may not restrict the content of their speech, the Supreme Court has held. In the words of the Court, laws that regulate speech must be "content neutral." Such laws must apply to all people, regardless of the message they want to get across. For example, in *Kovaks v. Cooper* the Supreme Court upheld the right of the government to regulate the loudness of sound trucks because the law applied to all sound trucks, regardless of the content of their broadcasts. In *Saia v. New York*, 1948, however, the Court struck down a law that gave public officials the right to decide who could use sound trucks. The New York law, the Court reasoned, allowed public officials to deny some speakers the right to use sound trucks based on the content of their speech.

All speech expresses a point of view, of course, yet the Supreme Court still allows its regulation. In *Greer v. Spock*, 1976, for example, the Court held that military bases could ban certain kinds of speech based on its content. Military leaders feared that partisan, or one-sided speeches that attacked public policy—especially about the use of military forces—could affect the morale of the men and women whose duty it is to carry out that policy, right or wrong. Seeing the role of the military as unique in American society, the high court ruled that military bases are not a public forum. Therefore, the content of speech on military bases can be censored.

An important factor the Supreme Court weighs in deciding the constitutionality of speech laws is

Distribution of religious material can be restricted in public places to specific locations, as members of the International Society for Krishna Consciousness learned in a 1981 Supreme Court ruling.

whether or not the restriction leaves open alternative channels of communication. An outright ban of speakers or protesters is more likely to be struck down than a law that limits the time, place, or manner of expression. For example, in *Heffron v. International Society for Krishna Consciousness*, 1981, the Court allowed the government to restrict the sale of religious pamphlets at a state fair to specific locations. This restriction was designed to protect the safety and convenience of the fairgoers. Because the law provided an alternative channel of communication—selling pamphlets from a booth—it was upheld. Had the law banned the sale of the pamphlets altogether, it would have been struck down.

Overbreadth

Some laws restrict more speech than is necessary for the government to achieve its aims of creating an orderly society. Usually such laws are struck down because they are overbroad. As Richard Conviser wrote:

> No law can withstand first amendment scrutiny if it could be revised so as to exert less restraint on

communication while still achieving its basic purpose; if a less restrictive alternative is available, the law is overbroad.

In *R.A.V. v. St. Paul*, 1992, for example, the Supreme Court struck down a Saint Paul, Minnesota, hate-crime law in part because it was overbroad. The law called for special punishment for any person who

places on public or private property a symbol, object, appellation [name], characterization or graffiti, including, but not limited to, a burning cross or Nazi swastika, which one knows or has reasonable grounds to know arouses anger, alarm, or resentment in others on the basis of race, color, creed, religion, or gender.

Robert A. Viktora, whose initials appear in the case name, had been convicted under this law because he burned a cross on the lawn of a black family that lived in a mostly white neighborhood. The Supreme Court did not doubt that the city had the right to protect homeowners from having crosses burned on their lawns. However, the Court believed that the city could achieve that goal and place less restraint on communication by enforcing trespassing, vandalism, and fire laws, instead of the hate-crime law. "Let there be no mistake about our belief that burning a cross in someone's yard is reprehensible," wrote Justice Antonin Scalia. "But St. Paul has sufficient means at its disposal to prevent such behavior without adding the First Amendment to the fire."

Vagueness

Laws governing communication are also unconstitutional if they are vague—that is, if they fail to make clear exactly what they forbid. Vague laws, the Court has held, can have a "chilling effect" on speech. They can discourage people from communicating even when their speech is constitutionally protected. For example, laws that prohibited

A hooded Ku Klux Klan member stands before a burning cross. Hate symbols like this were declared illegal by a Saint Paul, Minnesota, hate-crime law which the Supreme Court later said was too broad.

When communication becomes a public nuisance and violates the rights of others, it can be censored without defying the Constitution.

speech that "corrupts the morals of the youth" were struck down as vague because they did not describe in detail what kind of speech was restricted. Without detailed guidelines to follow, law enforcement officials must use their own judgment to decide if a crime is being committed. In such cases, the Court has found, the rule of law is replaced by the whims of public officials—the very thing the Constitution was designed to prevent.

The Supreme Court's rulings about time, place, and manner reveal a deep understanding about the process of communication. Self-expression can be practiced alone, but communication requires an audience. The act of communicating does not occur on some ideal plane. It occurs in the real world, at a certain time, in a certain place, often with other things going on. Sometimes communication receives the full attention of the intended audience. Sometimes it is ignored. Sometimes it intrudes on whatever else is going on. When the act of communicating becomes a public nuisance, infringing on the rights of others, it can be regulated, stopped, or even prevented. The First Amendment was designed to give communicators the protection of the law, not to place them above it.

4

Incitement

(Opposite page) Police carry away a demonstrator who took part in a barricade of city streets. Speeches and demonstrations that incite others to break the law can be censored or halted.

SOMETIMES SPEECH TAKES place at an appropriate time, in an appropriate place, and in an appropriate manner, yet it still infringes on the rights of others. In these cases it is the content of the speech, rather than the conduct of the speaker, that is the problem. For example, a person giving a speech might urge the audience to commit a crime—to attack police officers, burn a building, or even lynch a person.

The act of urging a person to break the law, any law, is known as incitement. All incitement cases involve speech, of course. Communication is the only way for one person to convince another person to commit a crime. The question the Supreme Court had to decide was whether such speech was protected by the First Amendment.

The first important incitement case heard by the Supreme Court involved the case of Charles Schenck, the secretary-general of the Socialist Party in America. In 1917 Schenck mailed leaflets to fifteen thousand young men. There was nothing unusual or dangerous about Schenck's conduct. Publishers sent magazines, newspapers, and circulars through the U.S. mail all the time. The time, place, and manner of Schenck's communication were appropriate. Still, Schenck was arrested.

At the time of Schenck's arrest, the United States was involved in World War I. To raise enough troops to fight the war, Congress had passed the Selective Service Act. This law allowed the military to draft, or forcibly recruit, men of a certain age into the army.

Schenck believed that U.S. involvement in the war in Europe was wrong, and he said so in the leaflet he mailed out. Schenck also believed that by forcing young men to fight and die for an unjust cause, the Selective Service Act violated a person's most basic rights. In his leaflet Schenck encouraged young men to break the law and resist the draft.

Because of the contents of his leaflet, Schenck was arrested. He was charged with breaking the recently passed Criminal Espionage Act. Accord-

Charles Schenck was convicted of espionage for urging World War I draftees to break the law and resist the draft. His case led to a landmark decision on the issue of censorship.

ing to the federal prosecutor, Schenck's message promoted disloyalty toward the armed forces. The leaflets, the prosecutor argued, made it more difficult for the army to recruit soldiers for the war. A federal jury agreed. Schenck was found guilty and sent to prison for his words.

Believing that his right to publish his views was protected by the First Amendment, Schenck appealed his conviction. His case reached the Supreme Court in 1919. It was the first important censorship case to reach the high court. In a unanimous decision, the Supreme Court upheld Schenck's conviction.

"Clear and present danger"

The landmark opinion was written by Justice Oliver Wendell Holmes Jr. First, Holmes established that the First Amendment is not absolute in its meaning. Using the now famous example of a person "falsely shouting fire in a crowded theatre and causing a panic," Holmes declared that even "the most stringent protection of free speech would not protect" some expression. Tested in the highest court in the land, George Hay's notion that speech was "exempt from all law" was found lacking.

Having established that the First Amendment has limits, Holmes devised a test to help the courts decide what kind of expression falls outside those limits. "The question in every case," the justice wrote, "is whether the words are used in such circumstances and are of such a nature as to create a clear and present danger that they will bring about the substantive evils that Congress has a right to prevent." In the Court's opinion Schenck's words created a "clear and present danger" that young men would resist the draft. Such resistance would be a "substantive evil," Holmes reasoned, because it could hinder the war effort.

'Watsa matter, don't you like freedom of speech?'

The phrase "clear and present danger" has been quoted so many times, both to support free speech and to limit it, that it has taken on a meaning of its own, beyond the context in which Holmes used it. Justice Holmes remarked on this tendency in his dissent to *Hyde v. United States*:

> It does ill service to the author of the most quoted judicial phrases regarding freedom of speech to make him the victim of a tendency which he fought all of his life, whereby phrases are made to do service for critical analysis by being turned into dogma [rigid beliefs].

People who are familiar with Holmes's famous phrase, but not with his entire opinion, often infer that speech must create a dangerous situation, such as causing a panic in a theater, to be restrained. This is not what Holmes wrote. According to Holmes, any speech that is likely to "bring about the substantive evils that Congress has a right to prevent" can be censored. Those evils include dangerous and violent acts, of course, but are not limited to them. Resisting the draft, for example, is a passive, nonviolent act, yet that was the very evil the Court sought to prevent by punishing Schenck.

"Imminent lawless action"

For fifty years, *Schenck v. United States* guided judges and juries across America as they tried to decide whether certain acts of expression met the high court's test for incitement. Then, in 1969, the Supreme Court narrowed the definition of incitement. To be considered as incitement, the

Speech that encourages immediate lawlessness can be censored, as in the case of antiwar demonstrators who are urged to commit arson.

Outfitted with a Klan robe and police-style helmet, Tom Metzger participates in a Ku Klux Klan march. Metzger was convicted in 1989 after inciting violence against two black men.

Court wrote in *Brandenberg v. Ohio*, 1969, speech must go beyond the "mere abstract teaching" that a law should be broken. It must be "directed to inciting or producing imminent [immediate] lawless action." It also must be "likely to incite or produce such action."

The *Brandenberg v. Ohio* decision has not been overturned or modified in the twenty-five years since it was written. Together with *Schenck v. United States*, it remains as the guiding test for incitement today. It ensures that words cannot be used to deprive another person of his or her rights of safety or property. For example, the leader of a violent group, such as neo-Nazis or the Ku Klux Klan, who urges his followers to commit a crime can be prosecuted for his words. This is exactly what happened to Tom Metzger, a white supremacist who was convicted in 1989 for inciting the beating of two black men in Oregon. Metzger's words were not protected under the First Amendment because they met the *Brandenberg v. Ohio* test of being aimed at "preparing a group for violent action and steeling it to such action."

Violence in the media

Recently some people have argued that some motion pictures, television programs, books, song lyrics, and even video games may be exempt from First Amendment protection because they, too, encourage lawless action. For example, members of the Combined Law Enforcement Association of Texas argued that the song "Cop Killer" by the recording artist Ice-T created "a clear and present danger" of "imminent lawless action." The song includes the lyrics, "I got my brain on hype— tonight'll be your night. Die, die, die Pig, die. F— the police! I know your family's grievin'. F— 'em!" Such lyrics, the police officers maintained, went beyond the "mere abstract teaching" that vi-

Recording artist Ice-T was the center of controversy after the release of his song "Cop Killer." Critics contended that the song's lyrics compelled listeners to commit violence against police officers.

olence against police officers was justified. The words, the officers argued, met the high court's test of "preparing a group for violent action and steeling it to such action" and could compel a listener to take actions he or she would not take in the absence of hearing the song.

In June 1992 the Combined Law Enforcement Association of Texas asked the distributor, Time Warner, to withdraw *Body Count*, the album that contained "Cop Killer," from record stores. Citing the cause of artistic freedom, Time Warner refused. Said Time Warner spokesperson Edward Adler:

> We absolutely deplore all violence and particularly violence against law enforcement officials. Nevertheless it is vital that we stand by our commitment to the free expression of ideas for all our authors, journalists, recording artists, screenwriters, actors and directors.

The Combined Law Enforcement Association of Texas called for a public boycott of all Time Warner products after the distributor refused to withdraw Ice-T's album from record stores.

The association of police officers then called on the public to boycott, or stop buying, all Time Warner products until the communications company withdrew the album.

Ice-T and many others within the recording industry disagreed with the organizers of the boycott. "The song isn't going to make somebody murder anyone," said Ice-T. "I'm exercising free speech." Martin Kent, the producer of *US: The Entertainment Magazine Show* for E! Entertainment Television, argued that society was trying to blame artists for its problems. The boycott, Kent wrote, was "a reaction to the symptoms of America's ills and not to the underlying problems."

On July 16, 1992, supporters of the boycott held a demonstration at Time Warner's annual shareholders' meeting. Charlton Heston, an actor and Time Warner stockholder, addressed the meeting. "I'm here to condemn this company's response to the growing clamor across the country against *Body Count*," Heston said. Quoting some of the most objectionable parts of Ice-T's *Body Count* album, Heston asked Gerald Levin, the president and chief executive officer of Time Warner, "to stop selling *Body Count* [and] donate the money you have made from it to the families of murdered police officers." Twelve days later, at Ice-T's request, Time Warner pulled the record from distribution.

Criminal intent

The case of Ronald Ray Howard, a nineteen-year-old Texan, suggests that the police officers who protested "Cop Killer" might have been correct about the role lyrics could play in the formation of criminal intent. On April 11, 1992, Howard shot Texas state trooper Bill Davidson during a routine traffic stop. Three days later Davidson died of his wounds. Howard said his actions had been inspired by the lyrics of a record album he was listening to as he loaded, aimed, and fired his weapon. Howard recalled:

> The music was up as loud as it could go with gunshots and siren noises on it, and my heart was pounding hard. I watched him get out of his car in my side mirror, and I was so hyped up, I just snapped. I jacked a bullet in the chamber and when he was close enough, I turned around and bam! I shot him.

The album Howard was listening to, *2PACALYPSE NOW* by Tupac Amuru Shakur, contains six songs that portray the murder of police officers. "They finally pull me over and I laugh," Shakur raps in one song, "Remember Rodney King/And I blast his punk ass/Now I got a murder case." Shakur often raps about using a nine-millimeter pistol, the same weapon Howard used to take Davidson's life: "Shot a cop/And watched him drop/Damn I said why did I/Have to use my 9?" Howard's attorney asked that the jury consider the effect of these words on the murderer's frame of mind as it decided what Howard's sentence should be.

The jury was not swayed by Howard's defense, sentencing the convicted killer to death. On the basis of Howard's testimony, the trooper's forty-three-year-old widow, Linda Sue Davidson, sued Shakur and his record label, Interscope Records, for gross negligence contributing to her husband's death. She said:

> I believe this kind of music can have a definite influence on people's behavior. Ron Howard may have pulled the trigger, but I think Tupac, Interscope and Time Warner share in the guilt for Bill's death and they should take responsibility for their actions.

Shakur's lawyers claimed immunity from legal action under the First Amendment. Davidson's lawyers argued that Shakur's recording is not protected speech because it meets the test for incitement. Regardless of the outcome of the suit, the fact that Howard himself—the only person who truly knows what was in his mind as he formed his intent to kill—said that the lyrics incited him to lawlessness remains a grim testament to the power of words.

Davidson's murder is not the only crime to raise questions about the free flow of violent expression in society. One of the most troubling cases linked to violent expression occurred in Great Britain in 1993. Two eleven-year-old boys abducted a two-year-old boy, doused him with paint, beat him to death, and left him on a railway line. The murder bore a chilling resemblance to scenes from *Child's Play 3*, a movie that one of the killer's fathers had rented. Searching for a reason why the two boys would commit such a violent crime, the judge in the case, Michael Morland, said, "It is not for me to pass judgment on their upbringing, but I suspect that exposure to violent video films may in part be an explanation."

"A culture of violence"

Alarmed by the toddler's murder and a general rise in violent crime in Great Britain, some members of Parliament believe that censorship of violent programming might be required. Calling for limits on "slasher movies" and "video nasties," David Alton, a member of the House of Commons, declared, "Many of the homes in the United Kingdom are increasingly saturated by a culture of violence disseminated by television, video and computer." British prime minister John Major stopped short of calling for a governmental ban, but he urged broadcasters to curb their "relentless diet of violence."

Like their British counterparts, many American lawmakers believe that televised violence must be controlled. In December 1993 Senator Byron Dorgan, a Democrat from North Dakota, released a *TV Violence Report Card* that rated the number of acts of violence depicted in television programs. Dorgan reported that an average of 10 acts of violence are shown every hour during prime time, from 7 to 10 P.M. Children are exposed to an average of eight times that amount in Saturday morning cartoons. The most violent cartoon shows were *X-Men*, with 129 acts of violence an hour, and *Teenage Mutant Ninja Turtles*, with 123 acts an hour, or one every thirty seconds. Senator Kent Conrad, also a Democrat from North Dakota, proposed a ban on violent programs from 6 A.M. to 10 P.M. "There is too much murder, too much mayhem, too much violence [on television], and it needs to be reduced," the senator declared.

Policing television violence

Senator Paul Simon, a Democrat from Illinois, cites research that links the viewing of violent television programming with increased aggression, especially among children. "We have over two thousand studies now," Simon told Terri Gross in an interview on National Public Radio in December 1993. He added:

> We have at least 85 that would have to be considered very substantial studies. The Surgeon General has warned us. The National Institute of Mental Health has warned us. Those who simply deny that there is any relationship between crime in our society and violence on the screen are ignoring all the research.

In 1993 Simon called on the television networks to reduce the amount of violence in their programming. Simon warned that if the networks

did not police themselves, then Congress would. Simon suggested setting up a government committee that would monitor television violence and issue an annual report, ranking programs by the amount of violence they contain.

Marjorie Hines, director of the Arts Censorship Project of the American Civil Liberties Union, an association of lawyers dedicated to defending the individual rights guaranteed by the Bill of Rights, declared that Simon's proposal amounted to censorship. "First of all, he is singling out a certain type of content in the arts and entertainment which he disapproves of, he disfavors," Hines told Terri Gross on the same program that carried Senator Simon's remarks. She continued:

> That's clear from the purpose of this government commission. It's another type of classification

A sarcastic banner condemns artistic censorship. Censorship opponents worry that the Simon proposal will limit expression in all areas of the arts and entertainment.

board, and although ratings and classifications are not as insidious [calculating] and direct a form of censorship as criminal penalties or direct orders by the FCC [Federal Communications Commission] or some other government agency, they have the same intent, which is to suppress, to intimidate, and to chill certain types of expression.

Television's impact on children

According to Hines, Simon's plan to form a violence committee would violate the First Amendment. Under the 1969 *Brandenberg v. Ohio* decision, Hines argued, speech cannot be suppressed unless it is intended to incite unlawful conduct. Hines declared:

That's the proper standard, because any lesser standard gets us into a realm where the government or private censors are arguing, "This speech, this book, this tract, this song, this TV show is dangerous because it fosters bad attitudes, it gives people bad ideas." And that's thought control.

Many people agree that certain television programs have a harmful impact on children, but they resent the efforts of public officials to limit television programming. Parents, not the government, should control what their children are exposed to, these critics argue. Wrote Jane Clifford, an assistant features editor for the *San Diego Union-Tribune*:

My kids don't need Senator Paul Simon or the Federal Communications Commission or the latest electronic device to watch over them. They don't need special-interest groups lobbying to get this show off the air or that show put on at a different time. They need me.

Parents can discuss the contents of programs with their children, voicing their approval or disapproval of what is shown. They can change chan-

"The children shouldn't be watching that show. I hope Congress bans it!"

nels or even turn the television off. "Monitoring TV violence and TV sex and TV stupidity is my job," Clifford continued. "After all, if I'm going to teach my children responsibility, I can't abdicate [give up] mine."

Responsible broadcasting

Lynn Marie Latham, cocreator and coexecutive producer of the television program *Homefront*, believes that parents must guide and shape television viewing in the home, but she disputes the notion that all responsibility lies with the parents. "Because we as viewers can turn off the set, it does not mean we as producers have the right to put anything we want on the air," Latham wrote in a *Los Angeles Times* article. Because television programs are carried into homes on the airwaves or by cable, Latham pointed out, television viewers are not making the same choices or assuming the same responsibility as people who rent videos or attend movies. "The television viewer has rights and interests the movie-goer does not," Latham said. Believing that "every story is full of messages, intended or not," Latham stated that broadcasters have a special responsibility to censor themselves. She added:

> We can't ignore what FCC Commissioner Nicholas Johnson pointed out many years ago: It makes no sense to guarantee advertisers a behavioral response from the audience while denying that the content of the stuff airing between the commercials has any effect.

In February 1994 Senator Simon reached a compromise with television executives. The networks agreed to sponsor outside monitoring of television violence. In June 1994 the four major television networks—ABC, CBS, NBC, and Fox—commissioned the Center of Communications Policy at the University of California, Los

Senator Simon's proposal to monitor television violence was accepted by television executives in February 1994.

Angeles, to undertake the job of counting violent acts on television. The results of this survey will be published in an annual report, just as Senator Simon proposed. "This marks a significant step forward," Simon said at a news conference. "What we're seeing here is the beginnings of a cultural change in the depiction and glorification of violence."

Some critics of television were skeptical, however, and warned that tougher measures—such as Senator Conrad's twelve-hour-a-day ban on violent programming—might yet be enacted. The American Medical Association (AMA), for example, called for more descriptive ratings systems for motion pictures and television. "It is not censorship. It is helping parents parent," explained Dr. Robert E. McAfee, an AMA trustee. Television executives disagree, however, and have vowed to fight against further censorship. If tougher antiviolence regulations are passed, they no doubt will be challenged in court.

5

Fighting Words

SOME SPEECH CAUSES lawless behavior by promoting it. The Supreme Court has held that such speech, known as incitement, can be censored. Other speech leads to lawlessness, not because it promotes it, but because it provokes other people to anger. Should such speech be censored, too? The Court has taken a divided view. In *Chaplinsky v. New Hampshire*, 1942, the Court ruled that a person who says things to provoke a fight is not protected by the First Amendment under those circumstances. A public speech is different, however. In *Terminiello v. Chicago*, 1949, the Court declared that when a public speech "stirs anger" and even "induces a condition of unrest," it is up to the government to protect the speaker from a violent response to his or her words.

In the Chaplinsky case the Court created the "fighting words" exception to First Amendment protection. The Court defined fighting words as personally abusive words that "by their very utterance inflict injury or tend to incite an immediate breach of the peace." In this case the defendant called a police officer "a goddamned racketeer . . . a damned fascist." Such a personal attack does not have the political, artistic, scientific, or religious value the First Amendment was

(Opposite page) An enraged college student screams at a police officer during a violent demonstration. When angry words become "fighting words" they are no longer protected by the First Amendment and are subject to censorship.

75

meant to protect, the Court reasoned. Lacking such merit, fighting words can be censored.

Speech codes

The doctrine of fighting words has been used recently by supporters of speech codes on college campuses. Citing the Chaplinsky case, advocates of speech codes argue that hate speech, or speech that slurs based on sex, sexual preference, race, religion, or ethnic background "by their very utterance inflict injury." Therefore, the authors of speech codes reason, hate speech is exempt from First Amendment protection. In an article entitled "Is There Ever a Good Reason to Restrict Free Speech on a College Campus?—Yes," Charles Lawrence, professor of law at Stanford University, wrote:

> Racist speech that takes the form of . . . insults, catcalls or other assaultive speech aimed at an individual or a small group of persons falls directly within the "fighting words" exception to First Amendment protection.

Many colleges have adopted codes to deter the use of hate speech on their campuses. Supporters of these codes reason that hate speech can be censored because it is intended to inflict injury.

Lawrence likens such remarks to a preemptive strike, or a wartime attack designed to disable an enemy army. Once a person has been attacked, the professor reasons, the injury has already occurred. No amount of debate can undo the damage the insult has caused.

A 1990 survey conducted by the American Council on Education and the National Association of Student Personnel Administrators found that 60 percent of colleges and universities had speech codes. Another 11 percent were in the process of writing and adopting such codes. The code adopted in 1989 by Brown University in Rhode Island, for example, prohibited students and faculty from subjecting "another person, group, or class of persons to inappropriate, abusive, threatening or demeaning actions based on race, religion, gender, handicap, ethnicity, national origin or sexual orientation."

Censoring abusive speech

In 1991, the president of Brown University, Vartan Gregorian, expelled two students for violating the school's speech codes during a drunken frenzy. "The incident was one of loud drunkenness, of shouting anti-Semitic, anti-black, anti-homosexual obscenities," Gregorian explained.

Benno Schmidt, president of Yale University, disagreed with Gregorian's actions. He maintained that the very reason universities exist is to promote a free exchange of ideas. "Universities cannot censor or suppress speech, no matter how obnoxious in content, without violating their justification for existence," Schmidt said.

Gregorian, however, drew a distinction between speech that is directed to the general public and speech that is aimed at an individual or a small group. "This is not a 'free speech' issue," Gregorian stated about the expulsion of the two

The Supreme Court has ruled that offensive speech aimed at an individual person is exempt from First Amendment protection.

students. "There is a difference between unpopular ideas expressed in a public context and epithets delivered in the context of harassing, intimidating, or demeaning behavior."

"Verbal tumult"

By distinguishing between words spoken in a public context and those uttered in a more personal context, Gregorian echoed the decisions of the Supreme Court. In the Chaplinsky case the high court made it clear that offensive speech directed toward an individual person is not protected by the First Amendment. In *Cohen v. California*, 1971, however, the Court ruled that similar speech directed toward the general public is protected.

Paul Robert Cohen had been convicted in California in 1971 of disturbing the peace because he displayed the phrase "F— the Draft" on his jacket. At the time of Cohen's arrest, the United States was engaged in the Vietnam War. Public opinion about the war was extremely divided. Debate over the merits of the war—and of the draft in particular—were heated. Protesters and police clashed on a regular basis. Antiwar activists routinely blocked traffic, took over college and public buildings, and burned draft cards.

The State of California maintained that displaying an offensive and divisive message about the draft at a time when passions about the war were at the boiling point constituted fighting words. Cohen's message, the state claimed, was likely "to incite an immediate breach of the peace." The Supreme Court disagreed. "While the four-letter word displayed by Cohen in relation to the draft is commonly employed in a personally provocative fashion," wrote Justice John Marshall Harlan in 1971, "in this instance, it was clearly not directed toward the person of the hearer [an individual]." Vulgar language has a place in pub-

Police officers routinely clashed with protesters during the Vietnam War. Police could remove antiwar activists from courtrooms but they could not censor protesters' speech in public forums.

lic discourse, Justice Harlan added: "Verbal tumult, discord, and even offensive utterance [are] necessary side effects of the broader enduring values which the process of open debate allows us to achieve."

In his opinion on behalf of the Court, Justice Harlan followed the reasoning of Justice William O. Douglas, who twenty-two years earlier had written the majority opinion in *Terminiello v. Chicago*:

> A function of free speech under our system of government is to invite dispute. It may indeed best serve its purposes when it induces a condition of unrest . . . or stirs people to anger. . . . Speech . . . may have unsettling effects as it presses for acceptance of an idea.

A condition of unrest

In the Terminiello case the high court held that the state cannot prevent speech just because it creates a fracas. The case involved Father Arthur W. Terminiello, a Catholic priest who had been disciplined by the church for his verbal attacks on Jews and other minority groups. Every time he spoke, Terminiello, who referred to Jews as "snakes" and "slimy scum," drew large, raucous crowds. Most people attended Terminiello's speeches because they agreed with his views, but others showed up to heckle the racist priest. Fights often broke out between Terminiello's supporters and his opponents. At one such speech the police decided to act. They arrested Terminiello for disturbing the peace.

Terminiello knew from experience that his words were likely to cause a fight, the prosecutor told the jury. His speeches created a clear and present danger of lawless action and in fact led to lawless action many times. Therefore, the prosecutor argued, Terminiello was guilty of incitement. The jury agreed.

Although Father Arthur W. Terminiello (second from right) was convicted of incitement, the Supreme Court overturned the conviction because Terminiello did not directly incite his audience to break the law.

The Supreme Court overturned Terminiello's conviction in a closely divided vote. The high court drew a clear distinction between speech that incites lawless action and speech that simply leads to it. To be found guilty of incitement, a speaker must appeal to sympathetic listeners to commit a crime. A person cannot be held responsible for saying things that might cause his or her opponents to lose their tempers and break the law. The role of the police, the Court declared, was to protect Terminiello, not to punish him for the actions of his opponents.

Justice Douglas's opinion guided the Supreme Court in another famous First Amendment case that originated in Illinois: *Skokie v. Collin*, 1977. Frank Collin, the defendant, was the leader of the National Socialist Party of America, a neo-Nazi group. Collin revered Adolf Hitler and called for "free speech for white people." He and his followers planned to assemble on the sidewalk in front of the Skokie Village Hall in uniforms that bore the Nazi swastika. The neo-Nazis would then march around on the sidewalk. Since nearly half of the residents of Skokie were Jewish, and many had survived the Nazi campaign to kill all

Jews, an attorney for the village, Harvey Schwartz, asked Cook County judge Joseph Wosik for a court order to prevent the neo-Nazi demonstration.

Heckler's veto

According to David Hamlin, one of Collin's attorneys, the argument used against Collin was the same as the argument used against Father Terminiello twenty-eight years earlier:

> The case which Skokie presented to Judge Wosik rested on a single, subtle twist of legal logic: if Frank Collin is permitted to demonstrate in the Village of Skokie, residents of the village will almost certainly break the law; therefore Frank Collin must not be allowed to demonstrate. . . . Skokie argued that the audience's reaction to the speaker could be grounds for censorsing the speaker.

The belief that speech should be censored because it might cause a hostile reaction is known as a heckler's veto. This term was coined by a University of Chicago professor of law, Harry Klan. It describes a situation in which a heckler, a hostile listener who creates a ruckus, is able to stop a speech he or she does not like, as if possessing the power of veto.

Frank Collin (second from right), leader of the National Socialist Party of America. Collin caused a stir in Skokie, Illinois, when he planned to march his neo-Nazis through the community, which has a large Jewish population.

Believing that Collin's actions would lead to violence, Judge Wosik granted the injunction. With the aid of the American Civil Liberties Union (ACLU), Collin appealed Judge Wosik's decision. In the appeal hearing another attorney for the Village of Skokie, Gilbert Gordon, argued that displaying the Nazi swastika to the Jews in Skokie amounted to uttering fighting words, because such an act would "tend to incite an immediate breach of the peace." Guided by the Terminiello case, the Illinois Supreme Court overturned Judge Wosik's injunction:

> We . . . conclude that the display of the swastika cannot be enjoined [prevented] under the fighting-words exception to free speech, nor can anticipation of a hostile audience justify the prior restraint.

Since Frank Collin did not plan to tell anyone to break the law, his actions did not constitute incitement. The fact that Collin's racist message might provoke a hostile reaction was not reason enough to censor him. Collin and his followers won the right to express themselves in Skokie.

6

Obscenity

IN THE UNITED STATES sex is a private activity, not only by tradition, but also by law. Consenting adults may engage in sex acts in private, but they are forbidden by law to do so in public. Laws against public nudity and lewd behavior also prevent people from performing sex acts onstage for the entertainment of others.

What happens, however, when such acts are performed before a camera? Does an act that is illegal onstage become legal because it is presented to the public in the form of photographs, a motion picture, or a video? The makers and sellers of sexually explicit materials, known as pornography, believe so. They maintain that since pornography is published, it is protected by the First Amendment. Others disagree. Publication does not magically transform illegal acts into legal ones, they argue. Pornographers must obey the same laws as everyone else; the censorship of pornographic material is simply an extension of nudity and decency laws.

Public decency may provide a reason for limiting the types of material displayed in theaters, galleries, or bookstores, critics of censorship laws contend, but it does not explain why there are limits on materials intended for private viewing at home. Just as the government respects the rights

(Opposite page) A demonstration against pornography is staged on the streets of New York City. A sign brandished by one of the protesters reads, "Freedom of the press is not freedom to oppress!"

85

of adults to engage in sex in private, it ought to respect their rights to make pornography part of their private sex life.

Pornography and the First Amendment

The first Supreme Court case to examine the relationship between pornography and the First Amendment was *Roth v. United States*, 1957. The high court drew no distinction between material intended for private use and that intended for public display. As far as the Court was concerned, if material was offered for sale, it was public and was, therefore, subject to governmental regulation. The Court did see differences between types of pornography, however. Not all material that featured nudity or sex was obscene, or objectionable, the Court held. However, the ruling left no doubt about the status of material that was obscene. "Obscenity is not within the area of constitutionally protected speech or press," wrote Justice William Brennan for the majority. Under the Court's ruling, a work that was found to be obscene by a judge or a jury could not be sold or circulated. Anyone caught selling obscene matter could be jailed, fined, or both.

The Court set forth guidelines to help judges and juries decide if a work was obscene. First, the Court defined an obscene work as one in which the "dominant theme of the material" had a "tendency to excite lustful thoughts."

To judge the work fairly, the Court said, jurors should use the standards of an average person. Just because a prudish person might be offended by a work did not mean it was obscene. On the other hand, just because a completely uninhibited person might not be offended by a work did not mean that it was acceptable. In addition, the Court said, jurors must consider the audience to

consist of adults and not attempt to judge the work by the standards of a child.

Jurors were also told to apply contemporary standards to the evaluation of the work. Tastes change, the Court acknowledged. A work that might have been considered obscene one hundred years before might be perfectly acceptable in the present. However, jurors should not try to guess what future citizens might think of a work. Their task was to judge the work by current standards.

Finally, the Court said, the work must be judged as a whole. A movie that contains two hours of sex acts and one minute of political commentary is not protected by the First Amendment, the Court reasoned, even though it contains some speech of political value. On the other hand, a five-hundred-page literary work that contains one page of sex cannot be considered obscene, no matter how much that page might "excite lustful thoughts."

The New York City Police Department confiscated thousands of pornographic publications after a 1957 ruling that obscene material was not constitutionally protected.

Not all of the justices on the Supreme Court agreed with the majority in *Roth v. United States*. Justice William O. Douglas issued a stinging dissent. Although Douglas previously had held that "obscenity and immorality" were "beyond the pale" of First Amendment protection, he attacked the notion that obscene speech can be censored without undermining the freedom of expression. "Any test that turns on what is offensive to the community's standards is too loose, too capricious [changeable], too destructive of freedom of expression to be squared with the First Amendment," Douglas wrote. He believed that the phrases used to describe obscenity were too vague to guide jurors:

> Under that test, juries can censor, suppress, and punish what they don't like, provided the matter

relates to "sexual impurity" or has a tendency to "excite lustful thoughts." This is community censorship in one of its worst forms."

Douglas's reasoning did not sway the Court, but it did encourage those who sought to challenge obscenity laws. In 1973, with both Brennan and Douglas still serving as justices, several obscenity cases, known by the lead case *Miller v. California*, were reviewed by the high court. This time Justice Brennan joined Justice Douglas in voting to strike down obscenity laws. The problem, Brennan explained in his dissent in *Miller v. California*, was that obscenity laws were overbroad and vague:

> After fifteen years of experimentation and debate, I am reluctantly forced to the conclusion that none

A passerby examines the window display at a bookstore that sells pornographic materials. The Supreme Court left decisions about what constitutes obscenity to local community standards.

of the available formulas, including the one announced today, can reduce the vagueness to a tolerable level.

The man who defined obscenity in *Roth v. United States* despaired that his definition of obscenity—or any definition of obscenity—was flawed, because each juror would interpret that definition differently:

> Any effort to draw a constitutionally acceptable boundary on state power must resort to such indefinite concepts as "prurient interest," "patent offensiveness," "serious literary value," and the like. The meaning of these concepts necessarily varies with experience, outlook, and even idiosyncrasies of the person defining them.

A "Right of the Nation"

Despite the misgivings of Justices Brennan and Douglas, the majority of the Court voted to uphold obscenity laws as constitutional. Once again the high court had to weigh rights in conflict. In an obscenity case the conflict is between the rights of individuals to express themselves in a sexually explicit way against the right of the community to maintain certain moral standards. The Court came down firmly on the side of the community. "There is a 'Right of the Nation and of the States to maintain a decent society,'" Chief Justice Warren E. Burger wrote for the majority in *Paris Adult Theater I v. Slaton*, 1973. He continued:

> We hold that there are legitimate state interests at stake in stemming the tide of commercialized obscenity. . . . These include the interest of the public in the quality of life and the total community environment, the tone of safety itself.

Burger and the Court did not accept the argument that censoring obscene expression posed a danger to the First Amendment. Writing for the majority in *Miller v. California*, Burger explained that the First Amendment was designed to protect

A protest march by members of Women Against Pornography, a feminist organization that views obscenity as harmful and exploitative.

the free exchange of ideas. Obscene material, by the Court's definition, lacks ideas. Therefore, censoring obscene material and censoring ideas were two different things. To argue otherwise, Burger declared, was an affront to the Constitution: "To equate the free and robust exchange of ideas and political debate with the commercial exploitation of obscene material . . . is a misuse of the great guarantees of free speech and free press."

Nor did Burger and the majority share Justice Brennan's lack of confidence in the ability of juries to decide whether or not a work was obscene. Juries routinely have to decide guilt or innocence guided by vague legal concepts such as criminal intent, premeditation, and actual malice. The task might be difficult, but that does not deter courts from trying to mete, or dole, out justice.

Indeed, in one of the most important aspects of *Miller v. California*, the high court ruled that obscenity was a question of fact to be determined by a jury, not a judge. The most a judge could do would be to issue a preliminary ruling that would give the police grounds to make an arrest in an obscenity case. Once the arrest was made, it would be up to a jury to decide the guilt or innocence of the defendant, based on whether or not the jury found the work obscene. As in any criminal proceeding, the verdict would have to be unanimous and beyond a reasonable doubt.

Defining obscenity

To help juries decide these important matters in obscenity cases, the Supreme Court expanded on tests set forth in *Roth v. United States*. Juries, the Court said, still must judge the work as a whole using the contemporary standards of an average person. To reduce the amount of vagueness in such cases, however, Chief Justice Burger offered a narrower, three-part definition of obscenity. First, he wrote, a jury must find that a work "appeals to a prurient [arousing or unusual] interest" in sex. Second, the work must portray sex in a "patently [obviously] offensive" way. Finally, the work must be found lacking in "serious literary, artistic, political, or scientific value." To be found obscene, Burger stressed, a work had to fulfill all three parts of the definition. If a jury was unable to agree that the work in question met even one of the tests, the work could not be censored.

For more than twenty-five years the decision in the Miller case has been upheld by the Supreme Court but attacked by free-speech advocates. For example, Nat Hentoff, a columnist for the *Village Voice* and the author of *The First Freedom*, argued that the Miller case broke the First Amendment's protection into many small pieces. He held this view because under that case there is no single, national standard for obscenity. Instead, the Supreme Court leaves up to individual juries the question of whether or not a work is obscene. Hentoff believed this was unfair, because it meant that a jury in one area of the country might find that a work is obscene while a jury in another area of the country might find that it is not.

Defenders of the Court's decision agree that there is no national standard for obscenity, but they believe this is a good thing. The United States, they argue, is too large and diverse to adopt a single code of obscenity. The beauty of the Miller decision, they say, is that individual communities can control the type of material sold within them. A small town in Iowa does not have to accept the same type of material that is allowed in New York City; the people decide for themselves what to censor and what to permit.

A nasty album

Both supporters and critics of the Miller decision point to a case involving the rap group 2

Two inquisitive boys peer into an adult bookstore and theater. Without a national standard, individual communities must set their own obscenity guidelines.

Live Crew as support for what is right and wrong about the Supreme Court's ruling. On June 4, 1990, a federal judge in Florida, José Gonzáles, ruled that the rap group's record album, *As Nasty as They Wanna Be*, which contains hundreds of graphic descriptions of sex, was obscene. After the ruling Broward County sheriff Nick Navarro warned local merchants to stop selling the album. Some complied, but record store owner Charles Freeman, who had sold more than one thousand copies of the album, did not. Two days after Judge Gonzáles's ruling, an undercover sheriff's deputy purchased a copy of *As Nasty as They Wanna Be* from Freeman. Two days later Freeman was arrested.

A few days later the members of 2 Live Crew also were arrested following a live performance in Fort Lauderdale, Florida. Like Freeman, the

Luther Campbell, leader of the rap group 2 Live Crew, was arrested after performing material from the group's album As Nasty as They Wanna Be. *The arrest followed a Florida judge's ruling that the album was obscene.*

members of the rap group each faced up to one year in jail and a fine of one thousand dollars if found guilty.

Guilty, not guilty

At his trial in October 1990, Charles Freeman did not deny selling *As Nasty as They Wanna Be* to the undercover officer. Instead, Freeman and his lawyers argued that the album was not obscene. As provided by *Miller v. California*, it was up to the local jury to decide if the album was obscene. The jurors found that the lyrics on the album met all three tests for obscenity set forth in the Miller decision. Freeman, the jury declared, was guilty.

Shortly after Freeman's conviction, the trial of the 2 Live Crew members began. The defendants did not deny speaking the lyrics in question, which had been witnessed and taped by undercover sheriff's officers at the performance. Instead, like Freeman's attorneys, the lawyers representing the group argued that their words were not obscene. The defense called in two expert witnesses who praised the performance. After deliberating for two hours, the six jurors found the rappers not guilty. "Representing a cross-section of the community as we do, we did not feel it was obscene," jury foreman David Garsow said of the performance. "We looked at the whole thing as a comedy," agreed Beverly Resnick, another of the jurors. "Once we heard [the words], they didn't bother us."

In the 2 Live Crew cases, two different juries reached two different verdicts over essentially the same material. The outcome of these trials points up the weakness of the Miller decision, maintain its critics. A work cannot be both obscene and not obscene at the same time, they argue. One person cannot be fined and another set free for trading in the same material.

Complex and "indefinite concepts"

Supporters of the Miller decision dispute the notion that the decisions involving 2 Live Crew reveal any weakness in the Supreme Court's decision. They point out the two juries considered two separate works. Although the live performance contained material from the album, it also contained jokes and commentary of a political and artistic nature that the album was lacking. The fact that jurors could distinguish between a constitutionally protected "exchange of ideas" and "the commercial exploitation of obscene material" is a testament to the ability of everyday citizens to grapple with complex and "indefinite concepts" and produce justice, the supporters of the Miller decision claim. It is also proof that the guidelines provided in this case work.

Of all the types of expression that can be censored under the Constitution, obscenity is the most controversial. In part this is because findings of obscenity are rooted in moral and reli-

gious beliefs that vary from person to person and from generation to generation. It is also because obscenity is highly commercial. A pornographer stands to make a great deal more money from his or her expression than does an antiwar activist, an abortion protester, or a racist hate monger. Pornography is a multibillion-dollar-a-year industry in the United States. With so much money at stake, the makers and sellers of obscene material will continue not only to produce their works, but to campaign for their acceptance by the public and to challenge the laws that would ban them.

Whether a person finds a particular work obscene depends largely on his or her moral and religious beliefs. These views change with each generation and further complicate the censorship dilemma.

7

Compelling Interest

THOMAS JEFFERSON ONCE said, "Given a choice between having a government without newspapers and newspapers without a government, I would not hesitate to choose the latter." Like others who had grown up under the prior restraint practiced by the British government, Jefferson knew firsthand that without newspapers to report and comment on its actions, a government can—and most likely will—abuse its powers. Jefferson and other architects of the U.S. government also realized that the citizens of a democracy had to be well informed about public policy if they were to govern themselves wisely. As James Madison, the author of the First Amendment, put it:

> A popular [democratic] government, without popular information [available to the public] or the means of acquiring it, is but a Prologue to a Farce or a Tragedy; or, perhaps, both. Knowledge will forever govern ignorance: And a people who mean to be their own Governors, must arm themselves with the power which knowledge gives.

The only means of acquiring information about the government, of course, is through expression—speeches, writing, and visual images. That is why

(Opposite page) Throughout history the media has helped keep Americans informed of public policy. Information about the government can be obtained through newspapers, magazines, and journals, all of which are readily available at newsstands.

Eugene Dennis and his wife ascend the steps of the federal courthouse. Dennis, a leader of the U.S. Communist Party, was convicted of advocating the overthrow of the government.

George Mason and others insisted on adding an amendment to the Constitution that would keep the government from "abridging . . . the freedom of speech and of the press."

While the First Amendment is an important part of the Constitution, it is not the whole document. It was not designed to create a society of "newspapers without government." Indeed, the First Amendment would be unenforceable, and therefore meaningless, without the social order made possible by government. As Chief Justice Frederick M. Vinson put it in *Dennis et al. v. United States,* 1951, "If a society cannot protect its very structure . . . , it must follow that no subordinate [lesser] value can be protected."

Because the U.S. government secures the rights and freedoms of its citizens, its ability to function has been protected by the Supreme Court, even when its actions conflict with the rights of speech and press. To prevail over First

Amendment rights, however, the government must show that it is serving an important public interest. In *Dennis et al. v. United States,* for example, the government stopped Eugene Dennis and ten other leaders of the Communist Party in the United States from using speech and newspapers to teach and advocate the overthrow of government. "Overthrow of the Government by force and violence . . . is certainly a substantial enough interest for the Government to limit speech," explained Chief Justice Vinson.

Preserving the government

Although the high court has placed a priority on the right of the government to preserve itself and to maintain the social order, it has warned public officials against going too far in suppressing speech and the press. Agreeing with the majority of the court to uphold the conviction of Eugene Dennis, Justice Felix Frankfurter nevertheless cautioned:

> The all-embracing power and duty of self-preservation is not absolute. . . . The right to exert all governmental powers in aid of maintaining our institutions . . . does not include intolerance of opinions and speech that can do no harm although opposed and perhaps alien to dominant, traditional opinion. It is better for those who have almost unlimited power of government in their hands to err on the side of freedom.

Justice Frankfurter realized that forbidding Eugene Dennis and other members of the Communist Party from advocating the overthrow of the government would have a restrictive effect on other speech. He wrote:

> Suppressing advocates of overthrow inevitably will also silence critics who do not advocate overthrow but fear that their criticism may be so construed. It is a sobering fact that in sustaining the conviction before us we can hardly escape restriction on the interchange of ideas.

Justice Felix Frankfurter agreed with the Supreme Court majority that upheld the conviction against Eugene Dennis but cautioned that such censorship could have a restrictive effect on other speech.

Tom Metzger reviews a copy of his newspaper, California Klan News. *The publication asserts its right to publish ideas that may seem radical or offensive to the government or general public.*

Even so, Justice Frankfurter agreed with the majority that preventing the overthrow of the government was a compelling enough reason to censor Dennis and his fellow communists. "The most tragic experience in our history," wrote Justice Frankfurter, recalling the Civil War, "is a poignant reminder that the nation's continued existence may be threatened from within."

Wartime censorship

Just as protecting the government from internal attack is a compelling enough interest to permit some censorship, so too is the protection of the government from external attack. "Security against foreign danger," wrote James Madison in the *Federalist,* paper number 41, "is one of the primitive objects of civil society." The government must have certain powers to protect itself from such danger. During time of war those powers include the right of the government to censor some speech. "When a nation is at war," wrote Justice Oliver Wendell Holmes in *Schenck v. United States,* "many things that might be said in time of peace are such a hindrance to its effort that their utterances will not be endured."

The reasons for censorship during a time of war are easy to understand. If a newspaper or a broadcaster were to reveal details about a military invasion, for example, the enemy could use this information to repel the attack. The power to wage war, the Supreme Court has stated, means "the power to wage war successfully." The government does not have to forfeit the element of surprise to preserve the freedom of the press.

The power to wage war successfully extends not only to secret military strategy, but to "every matter and activity so related to war as substantially to affect its conduct and progress," the Supreme Court held in *Hirabayashi v. United States.* As a result, the Court has given the government wide discretion in what it may censor during wartime. Broad-

casts from the battlefront, photographs of secret military weapons, even letters written by soldiers in a war zone—all of these forms of communication may be censored during a time of war.

The problem with giving the military the power to censor news about a war, critics of this policy contend, is that the people who decide what can be printed are the same people whose lives and careers are most likely to be affected by the news. Military censors have a built-in bias against the reporting of bad news about a war. During the Vietnam War, for example, military leaders routinely suppressed news about setbacks they had experienced in the battlefield. In one instance General William Westmoreland, the commander of U.S. combat forces in Vietnam, told Congress and the American people in November 1967 that the ranks of the enemy were "thinning steadily" and that the campaign had "reached an important point where the end begins to come into view." Privately, however, Westmoreland told President Lyndon Johnson that the war could go on indefinitely. The military also covered up wartime atrocities. For example, forces under the command of Lieutenant William Calley killed more than three hundred unarmed residents of the village of My Lai on March 16, 1968. News of the massacre did not reach the media and the American public until 1969. As a result of these and other deceptions, the American public supported the war long after military experts had concluded that it could not be won. Without accurate information American voters were unable to perform their civic duties knowledgeably, just as James Madison had predicted.

Barring the secrets of government

Even during the time of war, the government cannot censor speech or the press without showing a compelling reason to do so. During the Vietnam War, for example, the government tried to stop the *New York Times* and the *Washington Post* from publishing documents that had been stolen from the Department of Defense. These documents, known as the Pentagon Papers, described events that led to American involvement in Vietnam. The government, which had classified these documents as secret, argued that their publication would prolong the war and endanger lives. Based on this compelling interest, the U.S. Court of Appeals in New York issued an injunction, barring the *New York Times* from publishing the stolen information.

On appeal the Supreme Court struck down the injunction, stating that the government did not meet the "heavy burden of showing justification for the imposition of such [prior] restraint." For example, the Court pointed out that the period of

Headlines in the New York Times *call attention to the Pentagon Papers, a government study of the Vietnam War. The government argued that if the newspaper continued to print portions of the stolen study it would endanger lives and prolong the war.*

time covered by the documents had ended three years earlier, in 1968. Although embarrassing, the material in the Pentagon Papers did not appear to be especially timely or militarily sensitive. Concurring with the majority in *New York Times v. United States,* 1971, Justice Hugo Black wrote:

> The press was protected [by the First Amendment] so that it could bare the secrets of government and inform the people. . . . Far from deserving condemnation for their courageous reporting, *The New York Times, The Washington Post* and other newspapers should be commended for serving the purpose that the Founding Fathers saw so clearly.

Not all censorship is as obvious as the government's attempt to block publication of the Pentagon Papers. The government can protect its secrets simply by blocking access to people, places, or situations. During the Persian Gulf War, for example, many journalists and others believed the government was able to suppress negative reports about the war by blocking access to the war zone. The method the government used to suppress a free and unrestrained press, critics maintained, was the practice known as pooling. In this activity, soldiers escorted a small pool, or group, of reporters to the battlefront to observe the action. The soldiers limited where the reporters could go and to whom they could speak. The members of the pool were then returned to where a larger group of reporters was waiting. The pool reporters then shared the information they gained with other members of the media.

Justified restraint

In previous wars pooling was used to help reporters gain access to dangerous war zones. In the Gulf War, critics contend, pooling was used to limit the reporters' access to the combat zone. Because of this practice the picture that emerged of the war was tainted by the military's bias. "In ac-

Journalists could only observe the battlefront through pools and with military escorts during the Persian Gulf War. This practice was criticized by many of the reporters as an act of censorship.

tual operation, the rules proved highly restrictive," declared the Committee on Civil Rights of the Association of the Bar of the City of New York. "At best, stories were delayed. At worst, the presence of military 'minders' inhibited honest reporting."

The government denied that it had created pools to censor the press. Wrote Pete Williams, the U.S. assistant secretary of defense for public affairs:

> The press arrangements for the gulf war were not, as some journalists claim, the most restrictive ever in combat. Some limitations were necessary to accommodate a huge press corps and one of history's fastest moving military operations. Even so, reporters did get out with the troops and the press gave the American people the best war coverage they ever had.

Pooling was designed to give the press access to the battlefront, while ensuring the safety of both the reporters and the soldiers doing the fighting, the government maintained. The military did not deny that it reserved the right to review reports from the war zone, however. Such reviews were designed to prevent the press from accidentally revealing important information about troop locations, strengths, tactics, and missions. The military's media guidelines declared that news reports would not be censored for their "potential to express criticism or cause embarrassment."

Governmental secrecy

Although the press chafed under such restraints, most Americans, including many legal scholars, supported the restraints. Karl Tage Olson, a former editor in chief of the *Drake Law Review,* wrote:

> Operational security and the safety of United States forces are compelling interests justifying some restraint on media access and publication. Pool arrangements and reasonably administered security reviews are narrowly tailored to serve these compelling governmental interests and are, therefore, both constitutional and appropriate.

The need for governmental secrecy is important in this age of satellite communications, because information can be transmitted and received around the world within seconds. During the Gulf War, for example, the leaders of Iraq watched American news broadcasts to glean information about the progress of the war. Under such circumstances, Olson wrote, "The slightest bit of information intercepted by the enemy could tip American battle plans and cost lives."

In a sense, all constitutional limits on speech and the press reflect the concept of compelling governmental interest. Protecting individual citizens from slander, libel, fighting words, or false advertising; ensuring the right to a fair trial; preventing lawless behavior; securing the nation against armed attack—these and other vital interests have been found by the Supreme Court to be compelling enough to permit some censorship.

According to the Court, freedom and censorship can—and must—coexist. Without a free exchange of ideas, society will stagnate and die; without limits on speech, however, lawlessness will prevail. Perhaps Justice Frankfurter put it best in his concurring opinion in *Dennis et al. v. United States:*

> Freedom of expression is the well-spring of our civilization—the civilization we seek to protect and maintain and further by recognizing the right of Congress to put some limitation upon expression. Such are the paradoxes of life.

Organizations
to Contact

Accuracy in Media (AIM)
4455 Connecticut Ave. NW, Suite 330
Washington, DC 20008
(202) 364-4401

AIM is a conservative watchdog organization. It researches public complaints on errors of fact made by the news media and requests that the errors be corrected publicly. It publishes the bimonthly *AIM Report* and a weekly syndicated newspaper column.

American Civil Liberties Union (ACLU)
132 W. 43rd St.
New York, NY 10036
(212) 944-9800

The ACLU champions the rights set forth in the Declaration of Independence and the Constitution. It opposes censoring any form of speech. The ACLU publishes the quarterly newsletter *Civil Liberties Alert* and several handbooks, public policy reports, project reports, civil liberties books, and pamphlets on the Freedom of Information Act.

American Coalition for Traditional Values (ACTV)
100 S. Anaheim Blvd., Suite 350
Anaheim, CA 92805
(714) 520-0300

ACTV is led by evangelical Christian leaders who are united to restore traditional moral and spiritual values to American schools, media, and government. It supports parental involvement in selecting children's library materials and opposes pornography. The coalition produces videos and publishes the annual *TV Report*.

American Library Association (ALA)
50 E. Huron St.
Chicago, IL 60611
(312) 944-6780

The ALA supports intellectual freedom and free access to libraries and library materials through its Office for Intellectual Freedom. ALA's sister organization, the Freedom to Read Foundation, provides legal defense in important First Amendment cases involving libraries' rights to acquire and make available materials representing all points of view. The ALA publishes the *Newsletter on Intellectual Freedom*, pamphlets, articles, posters, and the Banned Books Week Resource Kit, updated annually.

Eagle Forum
Box 618
Alton, IL 62002
(618) 462-5415

This Christian group promotes morality and traditional family values based on the Bible. It opposes the depiction of sex and violence in media outlets such as television, films, magazines, and rock music lyrics. It publishes the monthly *Phyllis Schlafly Report* and the periodic Eagle Forum *Education Reporter.*

First Amendment Congress
2301 S. Gaylord St.
Denver, CO 80208
(303) 871-4430

This organization believes that a free press is not the special privilege of print and broadcast journalists but a basic right that assures a responsive government. It works to establish a dialogue between the press and people across the country, to encourage better education in schools about the rights and responsibilities of citizenship, and to obtain broader support from the public against all attempts by government to restrict the citizen's right to information. It publishes the *First Amendment Congress-Newsletter*, brochures, booklets, and educational materials.

Fund for Free Expression
485 Fifth Ave.
New York, NY 10017
(212) 972-8400

This organization is a collection of journalists, writers, editors, publishers, and concerned citizens who work to preserve freedom of expression throughout the world. It serves as the U.S. sponsor for the British publication *Index on Censorship*, which reports on violations of free expression. Its publications include *Off Limits: Censorship and Corruption* and *Restricted Subjects: Freedom of Expression.*

The Heritage Foundation
214 Massachusetts Ave. NE
Washington, DC 20002
(202) 546-4400

This is a public policy institute dedicated to the principles of free competitive enterprise, limited government, individual liberty, and a strong national defense. It believes that national security concerns justify limiting the media. The foundation publishes a weekly bulletin, *Backgrounder*; a monthly magazine, *National Security Record*; and many other books and research papers. It has published as part of its lecture series a paper entitled *Why National Security Concerns and the First Amendment Are Not Compatible.*

The Media Institute
1000 Potomac St. NW, Suite 301
Washington, DC 20007
(202) 298-7512

The institute is a research organization that studies media issues. It conducts research on the relationship between the media and business, on new communication technologies, the First Amendment, and other media topics. Its publications include *Reporting on Risk, The Diversity Principle: Friend or Foe of the First Amendment?* and *Hispanic Media: Impact and Influence.*

National Coalition Against Censorship (NCAC)

275 Seventh Ave., 20th Floor
New York, NY 10001
(212) 807-6222

NCAC is an alliance of organizations committed to defending freedom of thought, inquiry, and expression by engaging in public education and advocacy on national and local levels. Its publications include *Censorship News* and *Censorship Matters.*

National Coalition Against Pornography (N-CAP)

800 Compton Rd., Suite 9224
Cincinnati, OH 45231-9964
(513) 521-6227

N-CAP is an organization of business, religious, and civic leaders who work to eliminate pornography. The coalition believes that there is a link between pornography and violence. It encourages citizens to support the enforcement of obscenity laws and the closing of pornography outlets in their neighborhoods. The available publications include summary of the *Final Report of the Attorney General's Commission on Pornography, The Empty Embrace, Evidence of Harm*, and *Pornography: A Human Tragedy.*

National Coalition on Television Violence (NCTV)

33290 W. 14 Mile Rd., Suite 498
West Bloomfield, MI 48322
(810) 489-3177

NCTV calls for boycotts against advertisers of certain shows as a way to reduce violence on television. The coalition believes violence in the media increases violence in America. It monitors the number of violent acts in television shows. It publishes *NCTV News.*

Parents' Alliance to Protect Our Children

44 E. Tacoma Ave.
Latrobe, PA 15650-1141
(412) 459-9076

The alliance supports traditional family values. It advocates censorship in cases where it believes these values are being undermined. The alliance supports the inclusion of Christian teachings in textbooks and the labeling of records that contain offensive lyrics. It publishes position papers such as *Censorship in Education* and *Ratings/Labels on Recordings and Videos.*

Parents' Music Resource Center (PMRC)

1500 Arlington Blvd.
Arlington, VA 22209
(703) 527-9466

The PMRC was founded in 1985 to encourage placing warning labels on records with lyrics that promote sex, violence, and drug use. The center opposes censorship and instead calls for record companies to voluntarily print lyrics on the outside of record albums and to use a warning label on any album with explicit lyrics. Its most visible member, Tipper Gore, has published articles on record labeling in the *New York Times, Newsweek,* and other publications. Publications include *Rising to the Challenge.*

PEN American Center

568 Broadway
New York, NY 10012
(212) 334-1660

The center is a worldwide organization of writers, editors, and translators. Its Freedom to Write Committee organizes letter-writing campaigns on behalf of writers across the globe who are censored or imprisoned. It publishes the quarterly *Newsletter* and *Freedom-to-Write Bulletin*.

People for the American Way (PAW)
2000 M St., Suite 400
Washington, DC 20036
(202) 467-4999

PAW is engaged in a mass-media campaign to create a climate of tolerance and respect for diverse peoples, religions, and values. It distributes educational materials, leaflets, and brochures. It also publishes the quarterly *Press Clips*, a collection of newspaper articles about censorship.

Project Censored
Sonoma State University
Rohnert Park, CA 94928
(707) 664-2500

Project Censored publicizes news stories that have been overlooked by the major media. Each year it publishes a list of the ten most important censored stories, as well as a study of sensational stories that made the news but that the project feels were not noteworthy.

Reporters Committee for Freedom of the Press (RCFP)
1101 Wilson Blvd., Suite 1910
Arlington, VA 22209
(703) 807-2100

The committee is devoted to protecting the rights of the press and to upholding the First Amendment. It studies how subpoenas of reporters' notes affect their ability to gather news from confidential sources. It opposes closing criminal justice proceedings to the public and press. RCFP publishes *News Media Update* and *News Media and the Law* quarterly.

Women Against Pornography (WAP)
PO Box 845
Times Square Sta.
New York, NY 10036-0845
(212) 307-5055

WAP was founded by Susan Brownmiller, the feminist author of *Against Our Will: Men, Women and Rape*. WAP works to change public attitudes toward pornography by offering tours of Times Square, a major pornography sales area in New York City, and by offering slide shows for adults and high school students that show how pornography brutalizes women. It makes available a packet of information about the effects of pornography on American society.

Suggestions for Further Reading

The Bill of Rights and Beyond. Washington, DC: Commission on the Bicentennial of the United States Constitution, 1991.

J. Edward Evans, *Freedom of the Press*. Minneapolis: Lerner Publications, 1990.

————, *Freedom of Speech*. Minneapolis: Lerner Publications, 1990.

Elaine Pascoe, *Freedom of Expression: The Right to Speak Out in America*. Brookfield, CT: The Millbrook Press, 1992.

Bradley Steffens, *Free Speech*. San Diego: Greenhaven Press, 1992.

Works Consulted

Ellen Alderman and Caroline Kennedy, *In Our Defense: The Bill of Rights in Action*. New York: Avon Books, 1991.

Raymond Arsenault, ed., *Crucible of Liberty, Two Hundred Years of the Bill of Rights*. New York: The Free Press, 1991.

William Barbour, ed., *Mass Media*. San Diego: Greenhaven Press, 1994.

Edwin A. Burtt, ed., *The English Philosophers from Bacon to Mill*. New York: Random House, 1939.

Jane Clifford, "Mom Is Sole Watchdog Needed for TV Violence," *San Diego Union-Tribune*, February 19, 1994.

Congressional Quarterly, "'Buffer Zone' Ruling Bodes Well for Abortion Access Law," July 2, 1994.

Richard Conviser et al., *California II Bar/Bri Bar Review*. San Diego: Harcourt Brace Jovanovich, 1988.

Julien Cornell, *The Trial of Ezra Pound*. New York: The John Day Company, 1966.

William Dudley and Stacey L. Tipp, eds., *Iraq*. San Diego: Greenhaven Press, 1991.

Linda Greenhouse, "High Court Questions Scope of Florida Abortion-Clinic Ruling," New York Times News Service, *San Diego Union-Tribune*, April 29, 1994.

David Hamlin, *The Nazi/Skokie Conflict*. Boston: Beacon Press, 1980.

Nat Hentoff, *The First Freedom*. New York: Delacorte Press, 1988.

————, *Free Speech for Me—But Not for Thee.* New York: HarperCollins, 1992.

Knight-Ridder News Service, "High Court to Rule on Free-Speech Rights of Anti-Abortion Activists," *San Diego Union-Tribune*, April 25, 1994.

Milton R. Konvitz, ed., *Bill of Rights Reader*. Ithaca, NY: Cornell University Press, 1973.

Carlton Larson, "Should First Amendment Rights Be Unlimited?" Speech delivered before the City Club of Cleveland, Ohio, December 12, 1992.

Lynn Marie Latham, "All Stories Send Out Messages, Intended or Not," *Los Angeles Times*, August 25, 1992.

Don Lawson, *Landmark Supreme Court Cases*. Hillside, NJ: Enslow Publishers, 1987.

Bruno Leone, ed., *Free Speech*. San Diego: Greenhaven Press, 1994.

Felice Flanery Lewis, *Literature, Obscenity, and Law*. Carbondale and Edwardsville: Southern Illinois University Press, 1976.

Duane Lockard and Walter F. Murphy, *Basic Cases in Constitutional Law*. Washington, DC: CQ Press (Congressional Quarterly, Inc.), 1992.

Los Angeles Times, "Morning Report: Anti-Violence Campaign," March 9, 1993.

Terry O'Neill, ed., *Censorship*. St. Paul, MN: Greenhaven Press, 1985.

Chuck Philips, "Back to the Battlefront," *Los Angeles Times*, March 21, 1993.

————, "Rap Defense Doesn't Stop Death Penalty," *Los Angeles Times*, July 15, 1993.

———, "Rap Protest Heats Up," *Los Angeles Times*, June 13, 1992.

Reuters News Service, "Britons Seek Curbs on 'Video Nasties,'" *San Diego Union-Tribune*, November 26, 1993.

Reuters News Service and Associated Press, "16-Hour-a-Day Ban Urged for Violence on TV," *San Diego Union-Tribune*, December 16, 1993.

San Diego Union-Tribune, "Don't Gag Free Speech," September 3, 1994.

John Tebbel, *The Media in America*. New York: Thomas Y. Crowell, 1974.

David Van Biema, "Keep Your Distance," *Time*, July 11, 1994.

Marilynn Wheeler, "Violence Pervades Prime Time," Associated Press, *San Diego Union-Tribune*, December 18, 1993.

Index

About the Author

Bradley Steffens is the author of thirteen books for young people, including *Free Speech* for Greenhaven Press and *Printing Press: Ideas into Type* for Lucent Books. He has contributed essays, poetry, and plays to a wide variety of periodicals, including the *Los Angeles Times*, *San Diego Writers' Monthly*, *The Bellingham Review*, and *Minnesota Literature*. He lives in Poway, California, with his children, Zeke and Tessa.

Picture Credits

Cover photo by Frances M. Roberts
AP/Wide World Photos, 63, 64, 70, 73
Archive Photos, 61, 79
The Bettmann Archive, 10, 16, 29, 42, 87, 98
Engraved by Illman & Sons after a painting by George Romney; reproduced from the *Dictionary of American Portraits*, published by Dover Publications, Inc., in 1967, 27
Clark Jones/Impact Visuals, 78
Library of Congress, 8, 11, 14, 19, 21, 22, 30 (left), 35, 36, 41
National Archives, 26 (bottom), 30 (right), 31, 58
Laurie Peek/Impact Visuals, 84
Reuters/Bettmann, 40, 44, 56, 95, 107
UPI/Bettmann, 32, 39, 43, 49, 50, 51, 53, 54, 55, 62, 69, 74, 76, 81, 82, 83, 89, 91, 93, 97, 100, 101, 102, 105